FERRYBOAT FIELD GUIDE TO PUGET SOUND

BY ROBERT U. STEELQUIST

AMERICAN GEOGRAPHIC PUBLISHING

To Daniel Robin Hall Steelquist

Acknowledgements

The idea that became this book was conceived on a ferryboat en route to a meeting with the Puget Sound region's preeminent marine and environmental educators. I was serving, at the time as a member of the Puget Sound Water Quality Authority's "Education and Public Involvement Advisory Group." As a committee, we were developing strategies to create an educated constituency for Puget Sound, through traditional and non-traditional methods. On that bright, windy day between Edmonds and Kingston, my own effort at the Herculean task emerged. It is most appropriate that the members and staff of that group be acknowledged for their role in shaping my perception of the need for and means to bring the message of Puget Sound to the widest possible audience. To Tony Angell, Wendy Bolender, Wendy Pugnetti, Jim Kolb, Mike Reed, Doug Pierce, Tony Meyer, Bob Jacobson, Harriet Bullitt, Bob Hulberg, Richard Conlin, Kathy Fletcher, Nancy McKay, Karen, Johnson, Claire Dyckman and Sheila Kelly go my deepest thanks. The "EPIG" effort has spawned (through its "PIE Grant" process) projects comprising an astounding show of educational creativity. I hope that this book finds a home among them.

Another important contribution has been the enthusiasm and encouragement for the project shown by my publishers, American Geographic, where Mark Thompson and Barbara Fifer labored to fit yet another project into an already tight publishing schedule. I also thank Donna DeShazo and Stephen Whitney of Mountaineers Books for their support in shaping the early development of the manuscript. Lane Morgan improved the manuscript with her insightful comments. Laurel Black and Len Eckel have made the book better with their contributions.

Valuable technical assistance was given by Tom Terich, Jim Walton, Marilyn Dahlheim, Steve Jeffries, John Calambokidis and Steve Speich. I gained considerable insight from the comments and observations of uncounted and unnamed ferry crewmembers and fellow-travelers who shared their sightings, anecdotes and unanimous approval of the book-in-progress.

Finally, I would like to thank my family—Jenny, Peter and Daniel—for their patience while this project kept me away from the demanding role as father to toddler boys. I thank them also for their companionship when the book brought us together, on ferries, on Puget Sound, doing what too few families do: teaching and learning together. Celebrating Puget Sound.

ISBN 0-938314-67-X

P.O. Box 5630, Helena, MT 59604
(406) 443-2842

William A. Cordingley, Chairman
Rick Graetz, Publisher & CEO
Mark O. Thompson, Director of Publications
Barbara Fifer, Production Manager

Design by Len Visual Design
Maps by Robert U. Steelquist and Barbara Fifer
Printed in U.S.A. by Thomson-Shore

American Geographic Publishing is a corporation for publishing illustrated geographic information and guides. It is not associated with American Geographical Society. It has no commercial or legal relationship to and should not be confused with any other company, society or group using the words geographic or geographical in its name or its publications.

CONTENTS

About the Author

Robert U. Steelquist is a naturalist, writer and editor specializing in the Pacific Northwest environment. In addition to writing six other books, he has worked as a trailhand and naturalist at Olympic National Park and director of the Arthur D. Feiro Marine Laboratory in Port Angeles. He is currently publications editor for the Washington Department of Wildlife. Mr. Steelquist, his wife and two sons spend as much time as possible in Blyn, Washington.

KEY TO LOGOS

These logos in the text on individual ferry routes alert you when to look for:

Natural features of the shoreline; geological effects

Human-built features of the shoreline: towns, buildings, wharves and docks

Moving water: fetches, currents, channels

Sites noted and named by explorers; other points of historical interest

Marine and shore birds

Fish and marine invertebrates

Marine mammals: seals, whales, porpoises, sea lions, sea otters

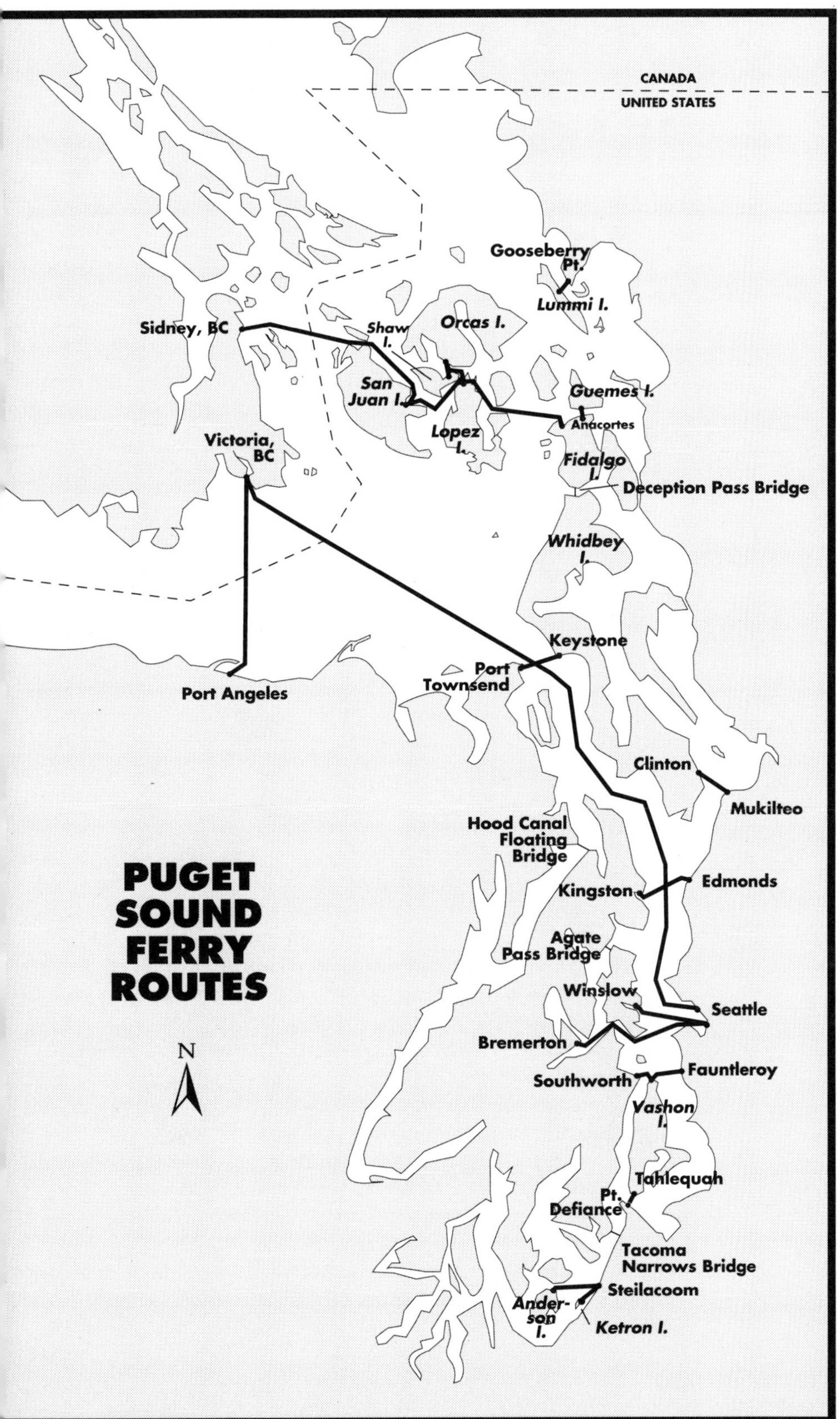
CANADA
UNITED STATES
Gooseberry Pt.
Lummi I.
Sidney, BC
Shaw I.
Orcas I.
San Juan I.
Guemes I.
Anacortes
Lopez I.
Victoria, BC
Fidalgo I.
Deception Pass Bridge
Whidbey I.
Keystone
Port Townsend
Port Angeles
Clinton
Mukilteo
Hood Canal Floating Bridge
PUGET SOUND FERRY ROUTES
Kingston
Edmonds
Agate Pass Bridge
Winslow
Seattle
Bremerton
N
Southworth
Fauntleroy
Vashon I.
Tahlequah
Pt. Defiance
Tacoma Narrows Bridge
Steilacoom
Anderson I.
Ketron I.

INTRODUCTION

In the spring of 1792, the HMS *Discovery* and its tender *Chatham* entered what we now know as Puget Sound. Aboard was Archibald Menzies, a naturalist on the Vancouver expedition, eager to discover new plant and animal species and to shine the dim light of 18th century science on the Northwest Coast. Menzies was a trained observer with a critical eye for new environments, and the Sound's first visiting naturalist.

From the water, he observed seabirds, mammals, fishes and plants. He took careful note of the weather, tide movement, and shore geology. And, whenever he had the opportunity, he stepped ashore to probe the forests and dunes that line the water's edge. In all, a remarkable picture emerged from his unique perspective, one in which he felt "regaled with a salubrious & vivifying air."

Vancouver's objective was to chart an uncharted shore, quell rumors of a fabled Northwest Passage and establish a British presence. As the vessels rolled in the swells and creaked in the wind, the lush green forests, distantly rising mountains and uniformly gray water—to this day all familiar characteristics of Puget Sound—revealed themselves to his party.

Vancouver wrote:

"The forest trees, and the several shades of verdure that covered the hills, gradually decreased in point of beauty, until they became invisible; when the perpetual clothing of snow commenced, which seemed to form a horizontal line from north to south along this range of rugged mountains, from whose summit mount Rainier rose conspicuously, and seemed as much elevated above them as they were above the level of the sea; the whole producing a most grand, picturesque effect."

His perceptions were based as much on his vantage point—aboard ship—as on the country that lay before him. From the ships and ships' boats, Vancouver and his officers surveyed the Puget Sound coast and gave names to many of the features that we know today. In addition, they surmised the nature of the country inland from Puget Sound, estimated its resources, and evaluated its potential as a future seat of what they knew as civilization.

It is remarkable how much they were able to discern simply by looking at the land from the water. And while it would be at least a century before some of the country they saw was visited, described and fully appreciated by overland observers, the picture of the Puget Sound country that emerged through their journals is surprisingly faithful.

Two centuries have passed since Vancouver's time. Although time has brought radical transformation to the face of the Puget Sound landscape, many of the features that Vancouver and Menzies saw and named remain recognizable. The captain and the ship's naturalist probably would recall many of the points, harbors and passageways were they able to see them today.

One reason is that much of the shore remains undeveloped. The view toward land from many points gives little evidence of the "Pugetopolis" that sprawls across the upland. Only where cities spill over the hills and onto the foreshore, where concrete and highrises become the dominant landforms and where seawalls and wharves obliterate the actual water's edge, do we get the sense that civilization has crowded upon the scene and altered it irreversibly. But most of the Sound's 1,700-mile coastline remains a darkened shore, where waves pour upon gravelly beaches in the shadows of stately conifers. On the distant horizon, the forms of Mt. Rainier and Mt. Baker loom through the haze, timeless in their dominance over the landscape. The wind still churns the water's surface and the tide still exerts its pull.

Along most of the shore, sediment movement, erosion and deposition continue to shape the land, despite our best attempts to check them. Beaches continue to harbor shellfish bounty. Estuaries

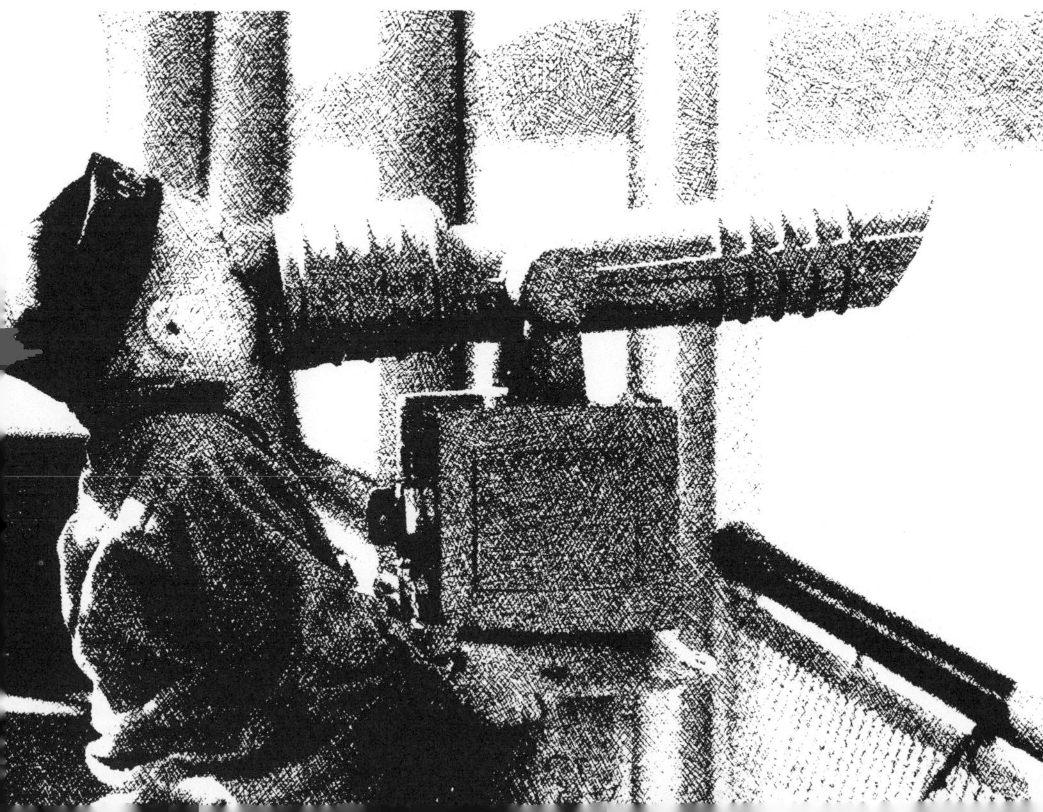

nurse hordes of salmon smolts. In the underwater meadows of eelgrass, in the floating rainforests of kelp, on the submerged ledges of reefs, and in the open waters of the Sound, a host of marine organisms live as though the dramatic events of 200 years of civilizing had not occurred.

This book seeks to introduce the natural history of Puget Sound, a treasure both diverse in its resources and singular in its importance to the economy and ecosystem of Washington's most populous region. It is written specifically for those who see the Sound first-hand—from the decks of ferries. And each year millions of travelers, whether residents commuting to and from work, or visitors seeing the Sound for the first time, experience it from just such a perspective.

Indeed, Puget Sound's ferries are an appropriate way to experience the Sound at its best. They ply many waterways that otherwise would be inaccessible to most of us. They enable us a vantage from which wildlife and nature's forces are vividly apparent. They reveal sensations of the marine world: the cries of gulls, the hiss of wind and the smells of salt air. Most important, they place us in the

picture, as active participants in the Sound's day-to-day life. They allow us to be ship's naturalists—with trained eyes, a rolling deck and an attitude of discovery.

This guide to the diverse processes and resources that comprise the Sound is intended for observers without training in oceanography or biology. It draws from an authoritative literature that has grown in recent years as concern for the Sound has grown. Use it in one hand, while—binoculars in the other—you travel any of the Sound's many ferry routes. Its purpose is to offer a fresh and personal perspective on Puget Sound, one gained only when we stand at the ship's rail and scan the horizon, breeze blowing through our sweaters or salty mists dampening our hair.

The book's opening chapters provide an overview of the processes that shape Puget Sound. These chapters connect causes to things that we see, rather than extend the horizon of scientific knowledge. They describe processes and phenomena you are likely to encounter on a cross-Sound ferry ride or that are conspicuous by their roles in Puget Sound's ecosystem.

In the chapter on wildlife, the accounts help you identify animals you see and understand their ecological settings. These accounts are by no means complete species guides or life-history accounts. The works that provide such information are listed at the back of the book. You can visit places with live collections of the Sound's many fishes and invertebrates: the Seattle Aquarium, the Vancouver Aquarium and Tacoma's Pt. Defiance Aquarium and Zoo. Other marine science and environmental education centers throughout the region also feature live collections or interpretive facilities that provide intimate encounters with remarkable animals. These facilities are listed in the appendix.

The second half of the book contains individual accounts of the ferry routes themselves and suggestions of things to look for. Generally, by reading the overview chapters first, you will be prepared. But don't worry if you've skipped ahead; the point is to see what's out there—you can always read about it later.

It is only fair to warn you that Puget Sound, like most of the world's oceans, can be full of surprises. You may see something inexplicable—even to an oceanographer or biologist standing at your elbow. Such surprises are a perpetual delight for those who observe nature—neophyte and scientist alike. Seeing such events clearly, remembering their details and later trying to ferret answers out of books or experts can be a challenge that creates pleasure far outlasting the brief encounter itself. With each mystery we solve, we are drawn deeper into a profound and personal relationship with the world around us.

Puget Sound is wilderness in the truest sense of the word—natural processes at work, an abundance of creatures not under man's control, an environment that offers opportunities for solitude and personal challenge.

Yet this water wilderness is under quiet siege. The sheer crush of people clustered into cities and scattered across the hinterland poses a danger to the integrity of an ecosystem that sustains its rich natural populations, which in turn sustain us. Coastal wetlands, essential habitat for many species, have been lost in the decades' rush to reclaim and develop the shore. As of 1985, more than 380,000 on-site sewage systems were in place within the Puget Sound watershed, contributing in some places to fecal contamination of the water. Toxic contaminants including PCBs, copper, lead, mercury and arsenic are present in localized areas and have been found in the tissues of fish, invertebrates and marine mammals. Nitrogen enrichment at river mouths is seen in extended plumes that stream far into the Sound before dissipating.

In its role as medium for dispersing products of the land—be they glacial sediments or human and animal sewage—the Sound has shown its limits. Some areas are more sensitive than others and their limits have been exceeded. The abundance and health of delicate organisms, some with economic importance and some without, tell us that changes are afoot, and that hardship can result. Experiences elsewhere remind us that great bodies of water accurately reflect the environmental and economic health of entire regions, that pollution and poverty are linked—if not in quantitative terms, then at least in that intangible, the "quality of life."

Puget Sound is a constantly changing reminder that a natural world still operates around us, among us, and in spite of us. That dynamism is cause for celebration as well as cause for commitment. The first step is to observe and experience the rich natural endowment that is Puget Sound and to gain a first-hand appreciation for its moods and its wild inhabitants. We must understand the profound influence the Sound has upon our otherwise complete domination of the land and recognize the effects that we have, individually and collectively, upon this great body of water.

We must understand thoroughly, before we can shape the personal commitment that lies at the heart of preserving the natural integrity of this great body of water.

PUGET SOUND ENVIRONMENT

GLACIAL LEGACY

Puget Sound occupies the central portion of a large depression basin that forms a lowland trough from British Columbia to the Willamette Valley of Oregon. Between the western rim—Vancouver Island, the Olympic Mountains, the Willapa Hills, the Coast Range of Oregon—and the broad uplift of the Cascade Range to the east, this depression basin shapes the principal drainage patterns of the maritime Northwest. In sharp contrast to the ranges that line either side of the basin, the trough is characterized by a gentle topography of rolling hills, with few outcrops of basement rock. As sea level rose following the last Ice Age, the valleys shaped by glacial ice were drowned by seawater, creating the Strait of Georgia, the Strait of Juan de Fuca and Puget Sound.

In a strictly historical sense, Puget Sound was the name given by Captain George Vancouver for the waterways south of the Tacoma Narrows, which were explored by Lt. Peter Puget. What we now call Puget Sound extends from Admiralty Inlet, where the sound narrows between the Quimper Peninsula and Whidbey Island, to the outspread fingers of Budd, Eld, Totten and Hammersley inlets in the south. In the most general sense, however, Puget Sound refers to the entire marine estuary system of northwestern Washington. Integral to those waters is the vast watershed that supplies the sound with fresh water discharged from 10 major and 14 lesser rivers. The watershed extends from the Skagit River, rising north of the Canadian border, to the Deschutes, which empties into the sound at Olympia. It also includes the steep river valleys of the eastern Olympic flank that drain into Hood Canal.

In the Puget Lowland, the surface features of the land have been worked and reworked over the last 50,000 years in at least four major periods of advance and retreat of Cordilleran glaciers. The most recent of these is known as the Fraser glaciation, which is divided into several lesser advances and retreats that occurred between 25,000 and 10,000 years ago. Signature deposits of gravel, sand and sediments have enabled geologists to reconstruct the events of the Fraser glaciation, a complex series of ice inundations, iceberg-dotted lakes and glacial floods. One element of this confusing array of transformations becomes clear: the recurring presence of an imposing lobe of ice in the Puget Lowland profoundly affected much of Western Washington.

The Fraser glaciation swept down through a structural depression between Vancouver Island and the Coast Ranges of British Columbia, fed by enormous valley glaciers pouring out of the mountains. As the massive tongue moved southward, it split around the the northeast corner of the Olympics—one lobe moved west and is known as the Juan de Fuca lobe; one moved south, forming the Puget lobe. The Juan de Fuca lobe occupied what had been a large river valley draining most of western Washington and southwestern and interior British Columbia, carrying the ancestral Fraser and Skagit rivers and others that now flow into Puget Sound.

The thickness of the ice varied. At Port Townsend, it is estimated to have been nearly 4,000 feet thick. At Olympia, near the southern tip of the glacier, estimates place the thickness at just above 1,300 feet. The Juan de Fuca lobe thinned as it stretched toward the ocean, forming an ice-shelf near the western end of the present strait. The vast glacier dammed river valleys, pooling water that backed up into the mountain valleys. The Elwha River evidently backed up high enough into the Olympic Mountains to spill over Low Divide and pour southwesterly into the Quinault drainage. Each of the major river valleys of the western slope of the Cascades contains large deposits of clay, laid in the relatively still waters of the glacial lakes. Many sites reveal steeply sloped beds of gravel, indicating river deltas built along the shores of the ancient glacial lakes. As lake levels rose and the

changing front of ice shifted, great floodplains were formed when milky water surged through lowland gateways to the sea. Much of the runoff from the Puget lobe flowed southward along the glacier's edge and through the Black Hills spillway into the Chehalis River Valley, making the Chehalis River, for a time, the Northwest's most powerful river.

The carving action of the glacier formed a series of deep basins that now contain Puget Sound. The deepest of these basins lies off Jefferson Point, to the south of Kingston. Water depth is 920 feet. Separating the major basins are shallower areas, known as sills, where water depth is considerably less. Two major sills in Puget Sound are Admiralty Sill, located just northeast of Port Townsend, where water depth is from 120 to 240 feet, and the Tacoma Narrows, where water depth is about 150 feet.

Above what is now sea level, the eroding power of the Puget lobe left the distinctive marks of glacial action on rock outcrops that rose in its path. Prominent outcrops in the San Juan Islands and on Fidalgo Island bear rounded tops and sides. Northern slopes often are relatively gradual, showing signs of abrasion; southern slopes are abrupt, the bluff-like appearance having been formed by glacial plucking. This pattern, typical of glacial landscapes, is the result of the dynamics of pressures exerted by the moving ice as it passes obstacles. Where pressure is high (the upstream surface) the glacier sole partially melts and lubricates. Where pressure is low (the downstream surface) glacier ice re-freezes, capturing blocks in the process.

As the ice advanced southward, it carried with it large quantities of rock plucked from what is now British Columbia. Upon the glacier's retreat, this debris was spread over the entire Puget Sound region. This blanket of sand, gravel and silt was laid down when glacial lakes, moraines and outwash plains formed at various stages of the glacier's growth and demise. Today's pale, layered bluffs that line Puget Sound reveal the thick covering of what was the vast ice-lobe's rock burden. Fine particles in orderly layers reveal the presence of standing water. Larger particles reveal the sorting effect of moving water. Glacial erratics, boulders of exotic composition, were left stranded as the ice in which they were encapsulated melted. These erratics show the movement of large blocks of ice or the drifting of icebergs. Layers of dense hardpan, known as glacial till, reveal the compressing action of the weight of the ice load itself on the material it overrode.

The abundance of glacial material throughout the Puget Lowland has significant effect on human occupation of the land. The soft, unconsolidated debris is relatively unstable. Loosened by rainwater, bluffs are particularly likely to slide. This represents a direct hazard to those who build on such slopes and an indirect hazard where the combination of waves, loose bluff material and Puget Sound's typical rainfall create a dynamic eroding shore.

Another very profound effect of glacial soils is their permeability and their role as a medium of groundwater movement. Generally, sand and gravel form soils that drain excessively, allowing rapid penetration and underground movement of rainwater, irrigation flows and other surface runoff. Glacial deposits form the principal aquifers throughout the Puget Sound region, storing the groundwater that much of the population relies upon for domestic consumption. In addition, once the water has penetrated the soil, it moves easily through the spaces between the coarse particles. Throughout a typical section of glacial deposits, lense-shaped layers of materials of various particle size are easily observed. Some of these layers consist of coarse materials, like sand and gravel, while others consist of compressed, impenetrable clay. Where groundwater encounters a layer of impermeable material, it moves along the surface of the layer. Because individual household septic systems add large quantities of untreated human waste to the land in such sites, the potential for groundwater contamination in glacial soils is high, and has in fact occurred as an alarming consequence of upland development. The fact that glacial deposits are both sources of domestic water and sites for domestic waste disposal creates the possibility of grave danger to human health. And even where human health is not threatened directly, the "overloading" of glacial soils from intensive on-site sewage disposal is an explicit threat to the Sound and its living resources.

WAVES & THE SHORE

When the massive lobe of glacial ice melted, seawater invaded and unleashed other forces to rework the Puget Trough landscape. Saltwater flooded basins in the rolling topography, beginning thousands of years of twice-daily tide pulses, surging currents and the chiseling of a fresh shore by waves generated on the surface of the great inland sea.

Today, the work of wave energy and the flow of currents is visible in each detail of Puget Sound's shore. Signs that this shore is constantly changing vary from delicate swash marks on sandy beaches to wide embayments, miles long. Particle by particle, soft bluffs erode into steep faces. Glacial deposits are sorted, moved and redeposited by the restless water, taking the graceful looping forms of sandspits and the inviting appearance of broad, gentle beaches.

Most of Puget Sound lies protected from wave forces generated in the Pacific Ocean. Ocean swells penetrate the Strait of Juan de Fuca, creating waves along the shores of the strait that gradually lessen with distance from the ocean. Their energy is dissipated by the continental shelf and diffraction over Cobb Seamount and Swiftsure Bank, large submerged features outside the strait's entrance. Nevertheless, shores of the Strait, the west-facing shores of Whidbey Island and the southwest-facing shores of the Lopez, San Juan and Fidalgo islands receive more pounding than shores protected inside Puget Sound. Rolling ocean swells are very noticeable to ferry travelers on the Port Angeles-to-Victoria run aboard the MV *Coho*. The 341-foot ferry pitches heartily in heavy seas, particularly near the center of the strait. In slightly more protected water, the Port Townsend-Keystone ferry rolls on ocean swells that have lost some of their strength because of nearby land masses and current turbulence at the Admiralty Sill.

In spite of its relative protection, Puget Sound is large enough for the formation of vigorous waves. Their primary source here is the wind. Once wind sets water in motion, uninterrupted expanses of water conduct energy very efficiently. Waves' effects are many. They can affect movement of objects floating in the water, drive nearshore currents, and mix waters of different temperatures or compositions. They also erode beaches and bluffs and redeposit material elsewhere.

Waves and Fetches

To understand the relationship between wave and shore, it helps to understand the nature of waves themselves. With the exception of waves generated by boat wakes (which cause significant damage in some areas), Puget Sound waves are most commonly formed where surface winds touch the water. Puget Sound winds are highly seasonal, with the strongest occurring in the winter. Winds may be localized, funneled by features of surrounding topography. For waves to form, a relatively broad expanse of open water is required. The area in which waves form is called a "fetch." The length and width of the fetch are very important in determining its wave-generating capacity.

To illustrate the development of waves, imagine a puff of breeze on perfectly calm water. First, a filigree of tiny ripples flows across the water, created by the friction of air moving along the water's surface. Such ripples form in irregular patches in response to turbulence and gustiness in the breeze. These waves, called capillary waves, are less than about 1.5 centimeters long ($^3/_8$ of an inch) and, without additional energy from the wind, would be dampened by the surface tension of the water. Because the ripples roughen the water's skin, and the wind continues to gust, more friction is created and the water surface becomes more irregular. With a slight chop, the water surface undulates, creating longer waves and vertical surfaces that catch the wind, like sails on a boat. The water is set in horizontal motion. The higher the waves, the more wind they catch, and the more water they can move. If waves become too high with respect to their length, they collapse, forming whitecaps and losing their energy in turbulence.

Because of irregularities in the wind and the heights and lengths of waves in formative state, such seas seem chaotic. Longer waves soon

Development of Waves

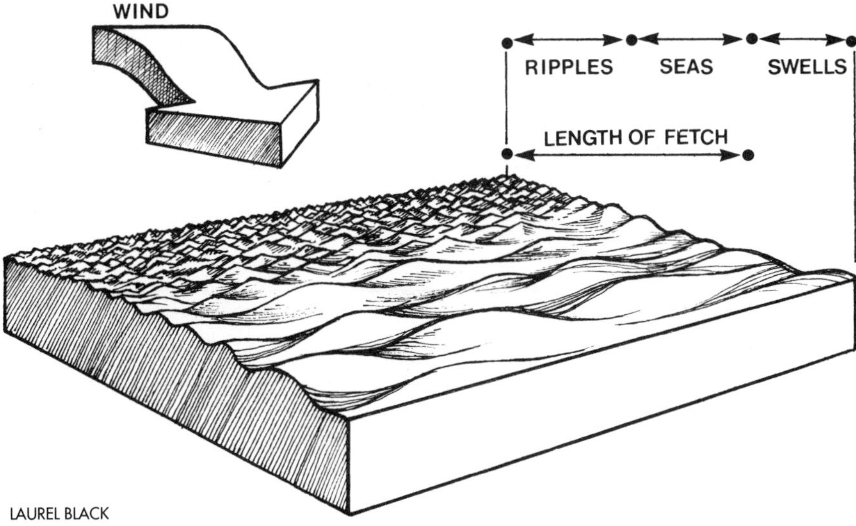

LAUREL BLACK

dominate smaller ones because they are more efficient energy carriers. They overtake and swallow smaller waves, absorbing their energy. As the waves are pushed by the wind over some distance, they begin to settle into regular patterns. Soon the waves organize into trains. At this point, they are what mariners call "seas." Thus, wind-driven waves form in an area of great disorganized turbulence and eventually sort themselves into series of evenly distributed pulses of energy, capable of traveling great distances without losing much of that energy.

In an ideal sea, wave trains would be fairly predictable. In nature, however, seas are made much more complex by the fact that winds are locally variable, fetches differ greatly in size and shape, shorelines are irregular, and local currents and tides influence water behavior. Puget Sound's surface, under stormy conditions, is a jumble of seas, composed of wave trains formed in different places, moving in different directions, canceling and amplifying each other in a multitude of ways.

Any body of water can become a fetch, whether sidewalk puddle or ocean. But the combination of surrounding topography, fetch configuration and seasonal weather patterns makes some bodies more predictable and more potent in producing wave energy. In Puget Sound, several notable fetches are responsible for wave patterns that have pronounced effects on the shores. The southern part of the Strait of Georgia creates waves that flow southward. Spit deposits at Sandy Point, visible to the north of the Lummi Island ferry, reveal the effect of the Georgia Strait fetch on local currents.

The Smith Island fetch, located at the confluence of Admiralty Inlet and the Georgia, Haro and Juan de Fuca straits, is the largest expanse of open water in the sound. Because of its size, and the fact that winds blow at one time or another from nearly all of the compass points, wave energy is fairly high along all its shores. The rocky shores of Fidalgo Island and the San Juans bear the brunt of waves generated by southwesterly weather systems; the soft bluffs of Whidbey Island, Marrowstone Island, and the Quimper Peninsula (Port Townsend)

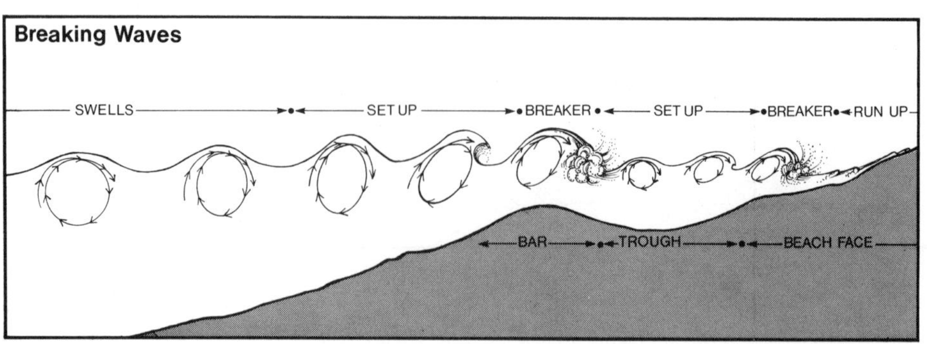

LAUREL BLACK

erode steadily as Smith Island fetch wave systems gnaw at them. These wave systems are easily observed from the Port Townsend-Keystone route and near the Anacortes end of the San Juan Island routes.

Possession Sound, the waterway separating Mukilteo and the city of Everett from Whidbey Island, also forms a significant fetch. Because of prevailing winter winds from the southwest, waves form in the central basin of Puget Sound and move northeast into Port Gardner (the Everett harbor). Landslides and erosion occur all along the bluffs south of Mukilteo and at Mission Beach, on the Tulalip Indian Reservation. Eroded material is deposited on a broad spit partially enclosing Tulalip Bay. This reach of the sound is crossed by the Edmonds-Kingston ferry route and by the Clinton-Mukilteo route.

South of Seattle, the sound is broken mostly into relatively narrow channels. Even though most lie generally in the direction of prevailing winds, wave energy is diminished by the baffle-like network of islands and peninsulas. Eroded bluffs and the orientation of spits suggest that waves originate mostly in the south. But winds are generally milder in the South Sound and the fetches are much smaller, so that wave energy is considerably weaker here than in the North Sound.

Erosion, transport and deposition: the sediment budget

Wave energy is felt most acutely when waves break on a shore. Here, all of the energy that the wave has collected over a wide area of fetch, and conserved in its motion, is delivered with a sudden punch to a very small area. In the form of waves, the energy can move large objects such as logs, boulders (and whole sections of sea-wall, when seas are particularly violent), loosen soil, sand and small particles of shore material and push them along the shore in fast-moving currents.

Erosion is at work. In areas of glacial till and outwash, high bluffs dissolve and collapse as waves undermine the bases of the slopes. Many areas of the Puget Sound coast are vulnerable to erosion and landslide. Because of high population densities in most areas of Puget Sound and the high value of scenic bluff property, planning agencies, developers and engineers have been challenged to identify areas of high risk and to build on such sites only with extreme caution. In spite of such precautions, slopes occasionally fail and property is lost.

Rates of erosion are slower along rocky shores, yet these too give way to the relentless force of water. Pounding water actually compresses the air in crack systems in the rock; whole blocks of rock can be pushed away from seacliffs by the air blast triggered by wave impact.

The mechanical principles of a breaking wave are relatively simple. Wave energy rolls through the open water the way a tire rolls over pavement, except that it has very poor traction. Individual water parcels travel in a circular movement, gaining only slight headway with each circle traveled. This motion, known as the wave orbit, remains relatively regular through open water. Sometimes wind pushes the top of the wave faster than the rolling motion of the orbit, causing it to separate and fall ahead of the wave. This is a whitecap. The froth is quickly gathered back into the wave orbit and the wave continues. When the wave reaches shallow water it is forced to change shape. As the bottom rises, the wave is pushed upward and shortened. The orbit becomes a tilted ellipse, standing on end. When the water depth decreases to about 1.3 times the wave height, the top of the orbit falls forward over the steepened face and the wave breaks, creating a rush of turbulence and a forward impulse. As the impulse wave climbs the beach, gravity overtakes its forward momentum and it slides back down the beach and percolates into the beach substrate. Retreating, it carries fine particles, which are stirred into the turbulence of breaking waves. In suspension, the particles move along a conveyor-like nearshore stream in a process called littoral drift or longshore transport.

Longshore transport is the flow of suspended sediments or bouncing particles in currents that run along a shore. These currents are driven mainly by wave action, although tidal flow and the motion of water entering from rivers or streams also play parts. Nearshore currents responsible for longshore transport are strongest during storms when wave energy is the most intense. During heavy wave conditions, longshore transport is visible as a murky plume of muddy water, moving slowly in the direction of waves. Often, feathery wisps of sediment-laden water traveling in small eddies are visible along the seaward edge of the nearshore current. Longshore transport is one of the great shapers of Puget Sound shoreline. In a single storm, thousands of tons of eroded material can be carried along a short stretch of shoreline, usually to a nearby area where the particles settle and form a spit, bar, shoal or beach.

Very fine grains of sediment, such as clay, are suspended in water. Heavier particles, such as pebbles and cobbles, bounce along the shore. Dislodged by a bursting wave, the pebble rolls seaward with the ebbing swash until it is carried landward by the force of another breaking wave. If waves attack the beach at an angle, the pebble's new position will be farther along the beach, in the direction of the movement of the waves.

Deposition. The ability of moving water to transport a load is based on its velocity. Slow-moving water carries only fine particles; faster water can carry larger ones. Current speed is a product not only of the energy that drives the current, but also of shore shape and water depth. Like rivers, which accelerate when constricted, nearshore currents accelerate as they are forced over or against a constriction. Similarly, as a river slows when it encounters a wide floodway or deep pool, nearshore currents lose velocity in deeper water or passing into larger bodies of water. As velocity decreases, sediment load is dropped, creating a buildup.

If we view the whole succession of processes that result from wave action striking a shore, a remarkable set of interactions can be observed. Sediment has its origin, its means of travel and its destination. The overall balance of these interactions is called the "sediment budget." Like the debits and credits of a bank account, there is a necessary relationship between erosion and deposition. Under natural conditions, bluff erosion serves to maintain beaches and spits. Without material to replace what erodes away in storms or blows inland, spits and beaches can disappear—or at least lose their sand. Viewed another way, sediment transport is the flow of particles from a sediment source to a sediment "sink." Sources and sinks are usually not very far apart. When you see an eroded bluff, try to discover where its sediment goes. Chances are, the beach or spit that is enriched by the bluff is nearby.

Because of the seasonal variation in the intensity of storms—and wave energy—sediment budgets vary dramatically from winter to summer. Most erosion occurs as a direct result of winter storm conditions. Many sandy beaches, like West Seattle's Alki Beach, visible from both the Bremerton and Winslow ferries, lose most of their fine sand during winter. The scouring action of heavy seas clears the beach down to its cobbles.

Beach profiles change significantly over the course of a year. Winter beaches are steep and narrow; summer beaches are flat and broad. The balmier days of summer bring the fine particles, along with sunbathers, boom boxes and beach balls.

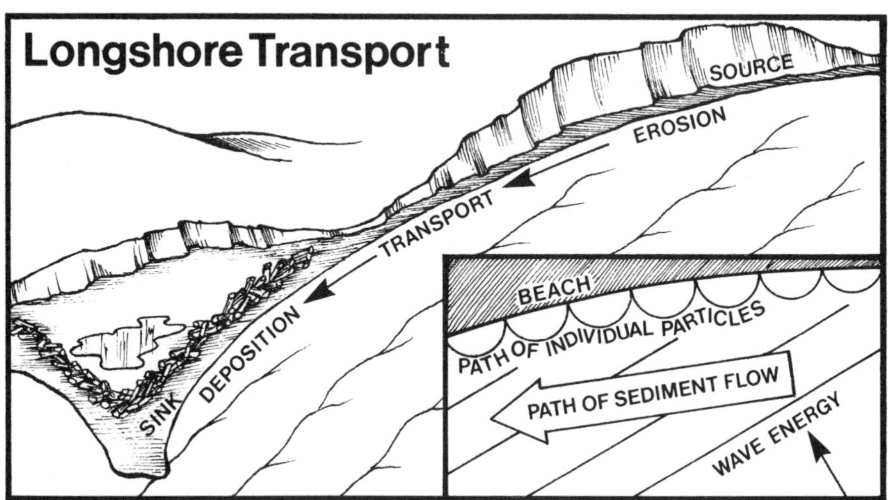

LAUREL BLACK

SHORES OF PUGET SOUND

Erosional features

Bluffs. Early explorers, including Captain George Vancouver, noted the pale cliffs of Puget Sound. Tan in color and frequently stained by iron oxides, these cliffs are composed of glacial and glacial-lake and -stream deposits of the Pleistocene. The bluffs reveal what geologists call a "middle-aged" coastline, where wave action over several thousands of years forced the retreat of a coast landward and created steep, faceted headlands. Along the water, Puget Sound bluffs are lined with cobble beaches—the heavier chunks of glacial deposits that the water cannot easily remove.

Many bluffs undulate gently along their shaggy tree-lined summits, evidence of the softly rolling topography that preceded the seawater flooding and coastal retreat.

Steep ravines that gouge into the bluffs as sharp Vs often are stream-eroded waterways that also existed prior to the coastline's retreat. Ravines with streams flowing through them into the Sound usually are skirted with a stream delta platform composed of gravel and sand transported from somewhere inland.

Bluffs frequently show signs of landslide. The most common form of landslide is called "slump." Here large blocks of bluff material move together as though contained in large slings. Slump blocks often roll backward slightly as they fall; on fresh sites, what used to be the bluff tops is visible as broken surfaces still adorned by plants. Bluffs also can "creep" downhill. The best signs of slope creep are trees that lean unnaturally outward from the bluff. Slowly, inevitably, the Puget Sound coast continues its retreat.

Banks. Another sign of coastal retreat in Puget Sound is the presence of extensive banks off many of the Sound's prominent points. Wave action—the most aggressive eroding force—is largely absent beneath the water. As a result, parts of former land masses remain as banks. Midchannel Bank, at the entrance to Port Townsend Bay, probably is a remnant of a formerly much longer Marrowstone Point.

Depositional features

Other signs of middle-aged coastlines are well developed depositional features such as deltas, spits, forelands, tide flats, and broad beaches. Puget Sound displays a textbook array of these features.

Deltas. River deltas represent sediment sinks for material eroded by glacial action or stream cutting, often located miles or dozens of miles from Puget Sound. In an undisturbed condition, they form important wildlife habitat. Because they consist of fine soil particles, larger deltas—such as the Skagit—have historically been of great agricultural importance. Several of Puget Sound's large deltas are no longer recognizable as landforms—those of the Puyallup and Duwamish rivers are now Puget Sound's principal seaports, and have been channelized, paved and industrialized.

Spits. Sandspits show the greatest diversity in form of all the depositional features. They may be simple, straight ridges of sand and gravel that rise above the water, formed by strong nearshore currents of one direction, or they may be elegantly curving bows and feathery plumes, revealing more complex current flow. Spits can connect nearby islands to mainland. They can circle around a point of higher land and enclose a brackish lagoon. Dungeness Spit, reportedly the world's largest, extends five miles into the Strait of Juan de Fuca. Nearby Ediz Hook, enclosing the harbor at Port Angeles, is also a long spit. Aboard the ferry MV *Coho,* passengers get a close look at the steep cobble of the Hook's tip as they enter or leave the harbor. When you look at the size of "fine" particles that make up Ediz Hook you get an appreciation for the strength of nearshore currents of the Strait of Juan de Fuca. Obviously, few spits of South Puget Sound will be composed of such coarse material.

Forelands are cusp- or triangle-shaped deposits of sediment found at the bases of blunt headlands where converging nearshore currents of opposite directions meet. Along Puget Sound, forelands form some of the most desirable real estate available. They are usually very scenic spots with broad beaches and flat building lots. Unfortunately, because they consist of gravel and sand, they make very poor sites for septic drainfields.

Forelands vary considerably in size. Perhaps the largest is Alki Point in West Seattle (visible from the Bremerton and Winslow ferry routes). Its enormous scale is due to very active sediment transport from bluffs as far south as Des Moines, on Puget Sound. Another very distinctive foreland is Flat Point, on Lopez Island. Flat Point juts into Upright Channel and is a prominent, low-lying feature visible from the ferry about 15 or 20 minutes out of Friday Harbor.

Tide flats are depositional features of the land/water juncture. Bays and inlets are relatively still, and large quantities of sediment are flushed into them by currents or deposited rivers. At low tide, a tidal flat is a broad expanse of oozing silt, carved with a network of branching runoff channels. Low-energy embayments throughout Puget Sound exhibit this remarkable shore type. Biologically, they form some of the richest habitat known.

Beaches. Puget Sound beaches are some of the most attractive landforms in Washington. To millions of residents, they practically symbolize the natural environment. For many, the word suggests solitude and bracing air; to others, sunshine and exercise. Yet for all of its allure, a beach in its plain technical definition is a zone of loose material subject to the action of waves, found below the reach of the highest tides. Beaches usually show signs of some sorting: wave and current action removes finer material, leaving evenly-sized larger particles. Because of the overwhelming abundance of sand and gravel in glacial deposits of the Puget Sound region, it should come as no surprise that most of Puget Sound's beaches are composed of gravel. Because of this, beaches are porous, with plenty of inter-particle space to form habitat.

A beach typically consists of a tidal terrace, a beach face and a backshore. The tidal terrace is a bench, exposed in the lowest tides, typically between six and 30 feet wide. It is composed of sediments temporarily stored along the longshore conveyor belt. Ripples or bars are often present. Frequently a prominent bar runs parallel to the shoreline, formed by sediments caught between the inrushing waves and the seaward backwash. Just shoreward of this bar is a trough, created by the scouring turbulence of breaking waves. The beach face is the familiar slope of the beach, over which the water's edge advances and recedes with the fluctuations of tide. Atop the crest of the beach face is the beach berm, deposited by the highest tides and wave action. On Puget Sound, the berm often is lined with driftwood. The

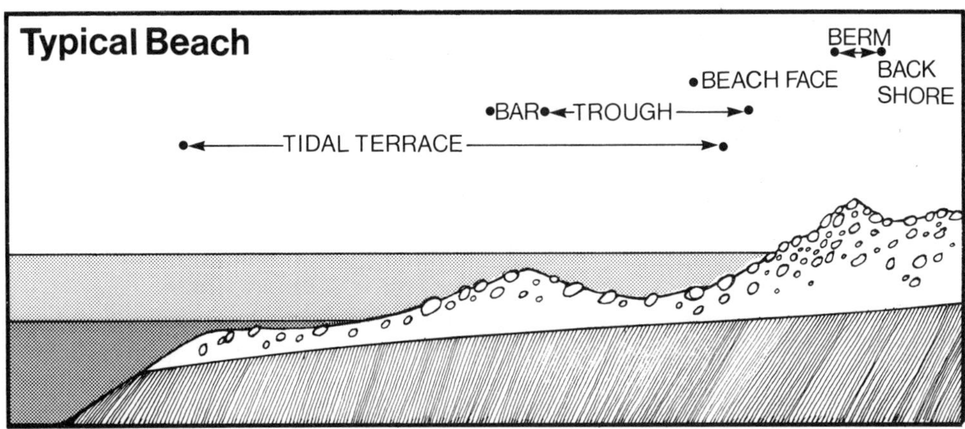

LAUREL BLACK

backshore comprises the zone landward of the berm. It may be low dunes covered with wild roses and ryegrass, or the faces of bluffs.

Built shores. Ever since human society took up residence on the shore, the dynamism of shore processes probably has caused some degree of concern. With the invention of real estate, deeds of title and property lines, living next to natural shoreline became a real hassle. Although property rights are supposed to have descended from God along with the other fundamental rights of human beings, no one apparently bothered to tell Nature. As coastlines inevitably retreat under the persistent forces of moving water, humans have little recourse but to accept the inevitable and retreat ahead of the waves.

In the Puget Sound region, human population has grown to 2.6 million in fewer than 200 years. Much of that population is close to the coastal zone. In urban areas, huge investments have been made in shoreline real estate for industrial and commercial purposes and, nearly everywhere else, Sound-front property has become increasingly valuable for residential use. In order to protect this pricey property, owners have constructed a wide variety of structures aimed at stopping the sea from its destructive trespasses. Many structures take the form of bulkheads or seawalls, usually made of concrete or timbers. Some property owners demonstrate considerable ingenuity, using such materials as tires, tree stumps and rock-filled baskets known as gabions. Most efforts fail.

The primary causes of seawall failure come from their supposed strength—their impermeability. Seawalls prevent the natural accumulation of debris at the feet of bluffs that create beach faces. Waves pound on the rigid wall, creating higher than natural scouring action. This undermines the seawall on the seaward side. As debris builds up behind the seawall from rain-loosened bluff erosion, pressure builds, tilting the wall seaward. Occasional high tides and strong storm-wave action scour behind the wall. It collapses.

Even when a seawall withstands the force of waves, it can create significant erosion problems elsewhere. As sources of sediment "dry up," beaches vanish. Without the cushioning mat of the natural beach, sloped to absorb wave energy, rates of erosion accelerate. And severing the longshore conveyor belt threatens depositional features such as spits and forelands that depend on steady supplies of fresh sediments to maintain their forms.

Another common method of protecting a shore is to construct a wall of large boulders, called rip-rap. Large sections of shore in Puget Sound are lined with rip-rap, often to protect railroad tracks and large pipelines. Perhaps the most extensive example is the shoreline between Meadow Point (just north of Shilshole Bay) and Mukilteo. These bluffs, now secure, probably were significant sources of sediment for sinks to the south, including West Point. Although no historical data are available to prove a connection, persistent slope failures north of Shilshole Bay may be a consequence.

Groins are short walls constructed at right angles to the shoreline, designed to trap sediment and create beach. These structures usually are very effective—in fact, too effective. But only temporarily. Groins interrupt sediment flow from source to sink, starving down-current beaches and promoting erosion by subtly altering the angle at which waves attack the neighboring down-current shore. Eventually, they promote erosion on the up-current side and defeat their purpose entirely. Rather than protect shoreline, they hasten its loss.

The final category of built shore is the dredged and jettied small harbor. A classic example of this modification is the harbor at Keystone, with its ferry dock and jetty. A small harbor is created to stabilize deposition and halt shoal formation where a given depth is needed to accommodate vessels. Like groins, jetties substantially alter longshore sediment transport, collecting sediment on the up-current side and starving the down-current shore. When the harbor entrance or basin is located up-current of the jetty, sediments actually are funneled *into* the basin. At Keystone Harbor, sediment flowing around Admiralty Head is trapped in the harbor and erosion on the down-current side of the jetty is severe. A four- to five-year dredging cycle has been established to remove sediment from the harbor basin and place it on the opposite side of the jetty. This costly solution bypasses the artificially created (and undesirable) sink, and restores the sediment (with some help) into the longshore conveyor belt.

HABITATS OF OPEN WATER

On Puget Sound, the dynamics of glacial sculpting, waves and currents created a diverse mixture of deep basins, turbulent sills, rocky headlands, cobble-strewn beaches, sandspits and broad mudflats. Nature met the challenge of this diversity through another process—evolution—in which a multitude of lifeforms steadily adapted to thrive in such widely differing physical environments. From an ecological standpoint, a great diversity of places—and the edges where they meet—creates a great diversity of habitats. When we look at Puget Sound as an ensemble of habitats, we can begin to fully appreciate its host of living creatures and the processes that link them.

A habitat is a place where an organism, or population of organisms, lives. The term also defines a community of many different types of organisms. It is a place that, because of its unique conditions, fulfills some or all of the biological needs of its living inhabitants. For a sedentary organism it may be a place to spend an entire life, feeding, resting and breeding. The habitat of an acorn barnacle is solid substrate near the tide line, where most of its life is spent stuck to a minute patch of surface. Swirling currents deliver food, carry off wastes and facilitate reproductive processes. Habitat for acorn barnacles is relatively common in Puget Sound. Wherever there is something solid (cliffs, cobbles, ship hulls, pilings and the like), and enough moving water, acorn barnacles will be found.

Habitat also may be a place where a highly mobile organism spends some crucial part of its life. Rhinoceros auklets are generally uncommon in Puget Sound, but locally abundant in a few places during the summer. Their nesting habitat is restricted to areas where soft, wind-laid soils covered with grassy turf allow them to create deep nesting burrows. Nest sites must be secure from terrestrial mammals such as dogs, cats, weasels and skunks, and they must be close to areas where large shoals of herring, sand lance, smelt and other forage fish mass or migrate. As it turns out, very few places in Puget Sound meet all of these requirements. Those that do—Smith and Protection islands, in the eastern Strait of Juan de Fuca—are of obvious importance to rhinoceros auklets and are designated national wildlife refuges to protect auklet populations of the sound.

As illustrated above, habitat may vary seasonally for certain organisms. When we describe such "part-time" habitat, we refer to it by its role in the life-history of the species—such as breeding, feeding or resting. Obviously, each is a necessary part of the organism's struggle to survive. We also refer to habitats by the names of organisms' life stages when they occupy that habitat. For example, "juvenile habitat" for salmon may be in estuaries near river mouths, where freshwater and saltwater mix and where the salmon can make the transition from life in a river to life in the sea. In the case of Dungeness crabs, adult habitat may be the sandy bottom near an influx of freshwater; habitat for its free-swimming larvae may be in the upper layer of water, where the tiny, ghost-like crabs drift among tide rips and other converging currents.

In the complex evolutionary legacy of a species, habitat requirements become coded in the genes. Some organisms have become highly adapted to very specific conditions. Bay pipefish, for example, are relatives of the tropical seahorse, and live in the cool waters of Puget Sound. Their shape, color and behavior are all adaptations that create a startling resemblance to gently swaying blades of eelgrass, an important marine plant found scattered around the Sound. The loss of eelgrass habitat would certainly doom the pipefish, whose evolutionary path has linked its survival to that of its habitat. Another, more conspicuous, eelgrass-dependent animal is the black brant. The diet of this small, migratory sea goose consists mainly of eelgrass. Flocks of thousands move through Puget Sound twice a year, en route to and

from their nesting grounds in the river deltas of Alaska. In Puget Sound, they rest and feed in large flocks, gathering strength for the strenuous migratory flights. Present black brant numbers represent a mere fraction of their former populations. The decline of this shy and beautiful goose over time is attributable, almost entirely, to the historic loss of eelgrass-bearing estuaries all along the Pacific coast. Thus, two very different types of organisms depend almost exclusively on the submerged eelgrass meadow habitat.

The open water

Puget Sound is a broad expanse of gray water, sometimes textured with waves, sometimes smooth. But the monotony of its broad surface, its steady horizon and monochrome appearance, give little indication of the intensity of living processes and the wealth of life-forms it contains. We tend to think of this huge volume of water as a homogenous vat of liquid, as uniform in its composition from top to bottom and side to side as bathwater in a porcelain tub.

In reality, the open water of Puget Sound is a complex mixture of widely varying habitats. The open water consists of distinct vertical layers where surface tension, light and dark, temperature, salinity, pressure and submarine currents create an astounding variety of physical conditions. In addition to habitats defined by these vertical gradients, physical conditions differ substantially along horizontal gradients, boundaries shaped by surface and underwater currents.

Oceanographers refer to a theoretical three-dimensional parcel of water as the water column. At its top may be a ferry boat, cutting the sea surface. Below are broad zones, the upper zone, light-filled; the lower, dark. At the bottom are the sediments, stirred by deep currents of cold water. Were we to descend in the water column without concern for our own physiological needs, we would observe a steady progression of changing conditions and a series of distinct habitats.

LAUREL BLACK

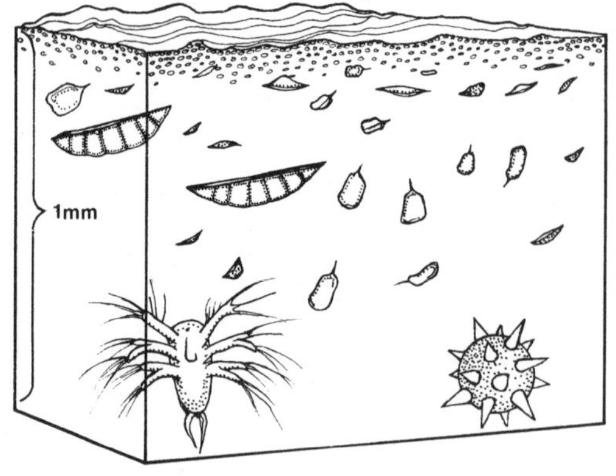

The sea surface microlayer

Until recently, little has been known about the "skin" of marine waters as a distinct and fragile habitat. In Puget Sound, studies reveal this to be a remarkably complex and important site for many physical, biological and chemical processes. The sea surface microlayer is comprised of the top millimeter of water in the water column. From the deck of a ferryboat it is, without question, the most visible of all habitats. Yet because of its extreme thinness (the thickness of about five pages of this book), and the diminutive size of its living inhabitants, it receives little attention.

Living occupants of the surface microlayer include bacteria, diatoms, very simple algae and minute larval forms of fishes and invertebrates. Some organisms adhere to the underside of the surface film itself; others attach themselves to tiny bubbles that cling to the surface film. The smallest attach themselves to organic and non-organic particle clusters that are part of the surface film. These particles originate in either the atmosphere (such as dust), or in the water column (as traces of organic substances of biological origin). Bacteria in the microlayer often feed on dissolved carbon that originates from the waste of plankton. Predatory plankton roam about the microlayer, voraciously gobbling smaller organisms, in turn being preyed upon by larger ones.

The surface microlayer thrives, like many other habitats, because it occupies a boundary between two very different environments. The influences of the atmosphere and sunlight, and day/night and seasonal cycles, are felt more strongly here than at greater depth. These dramatic fluctuations are responsible for a kind of revolving-door effect on bacteria and the minute plankton populations that use the microlayer—many organisms migrate to the surface during daylight and retire to deeper layers in darkness. Some migrate in an opposite pattern.

Surface tension on the water gives the environment its physical stability. Even on a white-capped sea, disruptions of the surface film are restored within fractions of a second. An effect of the surface microlayer sometimes can be seen on the water as streaming bands of smoothness. In these long slicks, surface films actually dampen the action of minute capillary waves, causing them to reflect light more evenly than on the more turbulent adjacent water.

Because of the biological importance of surface microlayer organisms to marine food chains, and the layer's physical and chemical importance as the major site of exchange between air and water, the surface microlayer is extremely vulnerable. The greatest threat to the surface microlayer as a habitat is the introduction of materials that settle on the water surface, particularly toxic and carcinogenic substances. Comparisons between urban and rural bays on Puget Sound reveal that considerably higher quantities of certain metals—including lead, copper, cadmium, zinc, chromium, nickel and mercury—exist in urban embayments, primarily from atmospheric deposition. In addition, the microlayer forms a vast trap for airborne hydrocarbons and oil-spill residue. Elsewhere on the world ocean, the microlayer has

The Water Column

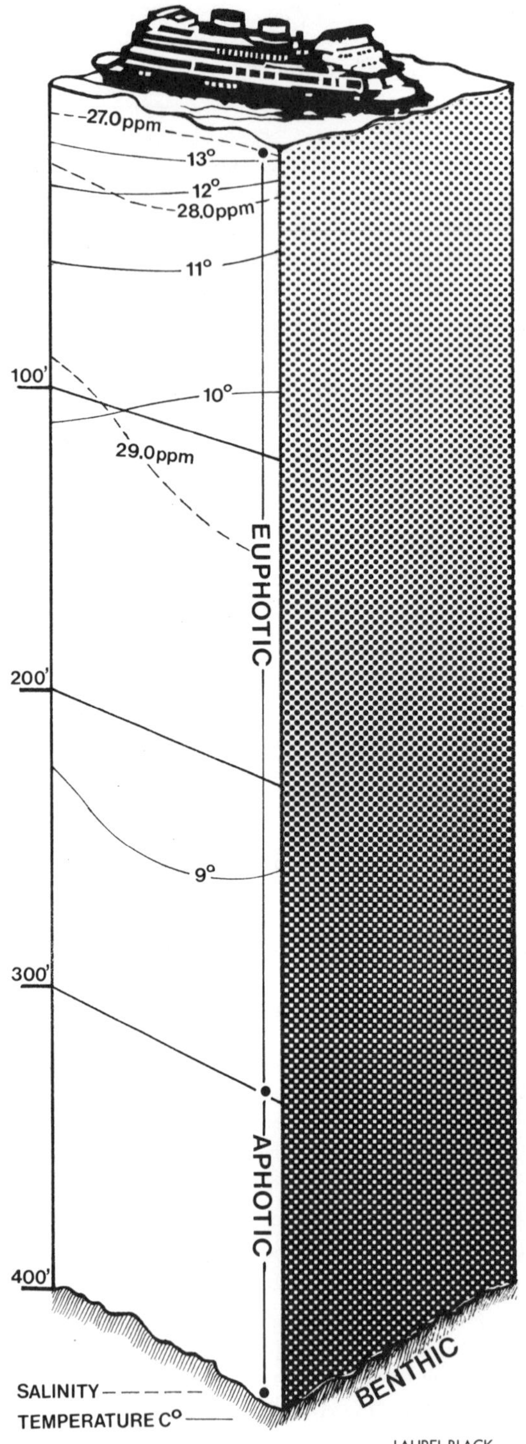

LAUREL BLACK

been shown to contain significant traces of pesticides—in Florida, DDT levels were more than 2,000 times higher in the surface microlayer than in subsurface water.

The euphotic zone

Our second stop as we descend the water column is in the shallow, sunlit region known as the *euphotic* (from Greek, *eu*—well; *photic*—light or lighted) zone. In Puget Sound, this zone extends to a depth of about 100 meters (or about the length of a football field). Because of the relatively shallow depth of Puget Sound, particularly its bays, inlets and channels, the entire water column may bask in filtered sunlight. These areas are extremely productive habitats that contain several unique communities, such as kelp beds and banks.

Metaphorically, the euphotic zone forms a vast green pasture. In terms of biological productivity in Puget Sound, it's the factory of the solar food chain. Blooms of phytoplankton erupt when conditions of light, turbulence and nutrient availability are at their optimum. Because of the horizontal and vertical boundaries between different great parcels of Puget Sound water, phytoplankton blooms are patchy. Following their explosive emergence, they drift around the basins of the Sound, pulled by tidal and flushing currents until the mixing action of the sills dissipates the blooms and time overtakes their short lifespans.

In the central basin of Puget Sound the timing of phytoplankton blooms coincides with the increasing sunlight levels and peak river runoff of spring. This burst drives the entire food chain. Diatoms form the majority of the phytoplankton of the springtime blooms. These are eaten by the herbivores, small copepods, euphausids and amphipods—similar in their role in the marine environment to insects on land. The first-order carnivores of the zooplankton include larger copepods, euphausids, amphipods, small jellyfish and others. These are eaten by juvenile and adult fishes of many species, which, in turn, are eaten by larger predators including diving birds, dogfish and salmon.

The aphotic zone

The eerie world of the lightless depths gives the marine environment much of its mystery. The bizarre adaptations of organisms that spend their lives in the aphotic zone (*a*—without; *photic*—light) long have fired human imagination and dread. Yet the same principles that govern other environments are at work in the depths. Many organisms are not particularly bizarre. Even for those that are, an appreciation of this extreme habitat can lead to an admiration of nature's great store of strategies that ensure the survival of species.

The aphotic zones of Puget Sound occur in the deep basins. Physical conditions include darkness, cold and extreme pressure. Adaptations to darkness include enlarged eyes, as in the case of the blacksmelt, a deepwater fish. Some cod, which freely roam above the bottom but feed near the bottom, employ a taste-bud–equipped barbel, a fleshy whisker on the chin, to aid in the search for food. Other sensory-enhancing adaptations in fishes include highly developed lateral line systems—pressure sensitive pores that run along the fish's side and detect movement in the water. Species of lanternfish have distinctive patterns of photophores, or light-producing organs, lining their sides. This enables the fish to recognize members of the same species. Subtle differences distinguish the sexes to facilitate mating.

Feeding strategies of the aphotic zone often include a preference for bottom-dwelling molluscs and worms. A large number of organisms act as scavengers, making a meal of the remains of anything organic that settles from higher in the water column. Several very desirable species of fish are deep-water predators. Ling cod and halibut roam near the bottom, feeding on fishes and invertebrates.

The benthos

The *benthos* is bottom (from Greek, meaning deep sea). The word "benthos" is often used also to refer to the collective group of organisms that inhabit the bottom (an instructive confusion perhaps, for it inadvertently equates the "place" with its "occupants," a unity we typically don't admit when we classify the world around us; ecologically, of course, habitats and their inhabitants are one).

The benthic zone refers to the water/land interface in water of any depth. Thus, the benthic zone is present whether the water body is a tide pool or a deep basin. The benthos, as a habitat, is a surface. It may be permeable, as in the case of a sand or mud bottom, or it may be impermeable, as in the case of rock. Most benthic organisms display adaptations related to their place on the bottom. These can include coloration that conceals them, and structures that hold them in a particular place or facilitate their movement on or in bottom substrate. Some of Puget Sound's most savored denizens are of the benthos: clams that range from the delicate native littleneck to the elephantine geoduck; Dungeness crabs and various species of sole and flounder.

Camouflage adaptations take a wide variety of forms. Tidepool sculpins, fish that dart among the pebbles and cobbles of many Puget Sound tidepools, appear mottled, with saddle-shaped patches of dark pigment. One species of limpet "sub-contracts" the task of camouflage, hosting the encrusting growth of magenta coralline algae, colonies of which also blanket the rocks of the bottom.

One very beautiful group of benthic invertebrates are the sea pens. Sea pens are distantly related to sea anemones, and inhabit sand and mud bottoms. The sea pen consists of two major body parts: a plume-like stalk covered with tiny fringed polyps, which resembles an ostrich feather, and a pickle-shaped base that is buried in the sand. Its tiny polyps capture fine particles of food streaming through the bottom currents.

Kelp beds

Kelp beds are to the marine environment what rain forests are to the land—seen from beneath they are great canopies of green inhabited by a host of other organisms. Like rain forests, they form habitats of great structural complexity. And also like rain forests, which absorb the physical forces of climate because of the bulk of material that comprises them, kelp beds absorb wave energy, reducing erosion on nearby beaches.

Bull kelp, classified as a brown algae, is the dominant member of Sound kelp beds. It consists of a long tapered tube with a bulb at its larger end. Long leaf-like fronds called "blades" are attached to the bulb. At its narrow end are stiff little branches called "holdfasts" attached to rocks, anchoring the kelp to the rocky bottom. Often, other types of algae grow on the floating bulbs of bull kelp the way moss grows on trees of the rain forest. Rockfish, greenling and perch congregate in kelp beds; the rocky bottom beneath is rich with sea cucumbers, sea urchins, sea anemones and other life forms.

Kelp beds are scattered throughout the San Juans and Puget Sound. The San Juan ferry passes many, including a large one along the north shore of Decatur Island in Thatcher Pass. Prominent beds are visible off Ediz Hook and near the entrance to Victoria's Inner Harbor, on the Port Angeles-Victoria route; off Admiralty Head, near the Keystone ferry dock; at Rich Passage on the Seattle-Bremerton ferry route; along the northern tip of Vashon Island on the Fauntleroy-Vashon-Southworth ferry route; and along the south end of Vashon Island and along the shore of Pt. Defiance on the Pt. Defiance-Tahlequah ferry route.

Banks

Ask any sport fisherman to name a favorite spot for bottomfish and, if he tells you at all, he is likely to name some bank. Even without a chart, you can make a reasonable guess at the location of an underwater bank by looking for a nearshore area with concentrations of birds, particularly gulls and divers. Birds will busily work the surface, noisily fluttering up and plopping down as forage fish rise to the surface. An approaching boat will scatter birds in all directions, including beneath the waves.

The productivity of banks is due to their shallow depth and the mixing of coldwater-borne nutrient-rich sediments. Sunlight reaches the submerged plateau surfaces, supporting large quantities of subtidal algae which create maze-like structural conditions. Forage fish congregate in large concentrations in these areas; their predators—lingcod, rockfish and halibut—follow. Banks are also important guideposts for migrating salmon.

Current rips

Sites of opposing current flow, known as convergence zones or tide rips, are also very productive habitats of the open water. Where large moving parcels of water meet, the surface will be marked with long streamers of foam and flotsam. Beneath the surface, plankton and small fish also can become trapped by the powerful physical forces. Gulls and diving birds frequently congregate in convergence zones. In northern Puget Sound, convergences are also the locations of most sightings of Minke whales, which cruise the water in search of shoals of plankton.

HABITATS OF THE SHORE

The intertidal zone

The intertidal zone vividly illustrates the principle that the interface between different habitats creates the richest kind of habitat. The intertidal zone is a world among two worlds: that of the land when the tide is out, that of the sea when the tide is in. Plants and animals that live here must be able to survive exposure to air and inundation by water, the extremes of climate, predation from air-dwellers and water-dwellers and the bursting energy of breaking waves.

Beaches. Cobble beaches are common throughout Puget Sound, a product of the glacial materials that blanket the whole region. The cobble beach habitat supports a wide diversity of organisms, mostly those that live beneath the surface among the cavities between rocks. The most useful organisms of the cobble beach are its hardshell clams. Common species of the Sound include heart cockle, horse clam, native littleneck, Japanese littleneck or Manila clam, and butter clam. Habitat requirements vary among the species: some prefer larger or smaller particles and each has a preferred station at or above the low-water line.

Native littleneck populations in Sequim and Discovery bays form most of the commercially viable populations remaining in Puget Sound. Siltation in most of the Sound has converted native littleneck habitat to butter, horse and Manila clam habitat. The natives now fetch premium prices.

Rocky shores. What is immediately apparent about a rocky intertidal community is its overcrowding. At low tide, the rocky intertidal community consists of broad swatches of mussels and barnacles and a distinct pattern of bands or zones of different communities. These bands correspond to wave-action intensity at different tide levels, tolerances of exposure to air and sunlight and the presence or absence of certain predators. Typically, zone systems consist of a splash zone, and upper, middle and lower intertidal zones.

Organisms living in the rocky intertidal zone must compete fiercely for space—places to attach themselves to the rocks, "stations" where they can feed on rich drifting particles in seawater or locations where they are protected from intense wave action. Mussels and acorn barnacles seem to dominate, but closer examination reveals pink patches of coralline algae covering many rocks (and even animals) in the tide pools; rockweed, a brownish seaweed with air sacs, grows in dense patches in the mid-intertidal zone. Bare spots occur where logs, pounding in the surf, have destroyed the communities of marine animals that resided there. Such spaces repopulate quickly.

Estuaries. Puget Sound as a whole is often defined as a large estuary: a semi-enclosed basin of marine water partially diluted by freshwater. But within the greater estuary are many smaller ones, where rivers enter the Sound and create localized conditions of salt- and freshwater mixing. These typically low-energy environments form the richest of all the intertidal environments of Puget Sound. Estuaries serve as large traps that hold nutrients, organic debris and sediments as they wash from the terrestrial environment into the marine. Because of the accumulation of nutrients, the biological productivity of estuaries surpasses that of nearly all habitat types except reefs and rain forests of the tropics. Broad expanses of mudflat nurture thousands of invertebrates per bushel basket of estuary mud. These nourish diverse higher forms, including fishes, mammals and birds.

Estuaries are critical nursery environments for young salmon, which often quadruple in size during their short stay. Here, they lose the color markings that blended them into the dappled background of stream bottoms and gain the silvery color that will conceal them in the open sea.

Estuaries are feeding grounds for millions of migratory shorebirds and waterfowl that pass through the Puget Sound region. At low tide, skittering flocks of western sandpipers, dunlins, plovers, and other long-billed and long-legged birds flow over the wide, tidal terrace pricking the mud for food. High tide concentrates them into dense lines along the beach where they continue the feast. Along the estuary shores, migratory geese and ducks feed and rest. During the winter,

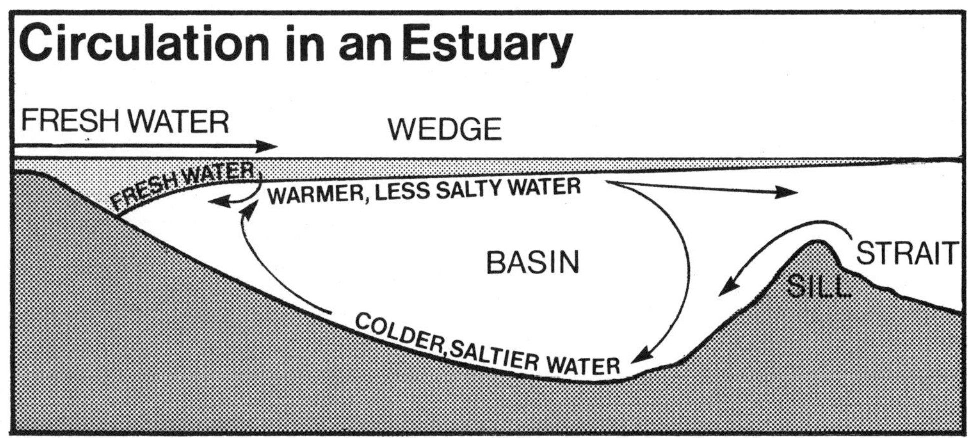

LAUREL BLACK

the relative calm of the estuary surface attracts great mixed rafts of grebes, scoters, loons and ducks.

Eelgrass beds. One critical habitat component of Puget Sound estuaries is the eelgrass bed. Unlike other seaweeds, most of which are forms of algae, eelgrass is a perennial flowering plant adapted for life in the marine environment. It forms underwater meadows that actually bloom and release seeds into the shallow, swirling tidal currents. Acres of waving eelgrass leaves provide food and complex shelter for many other organisms. Bacteria and minute algae thrive on the leaf surfaces. Tiny worms and other invertebrates feed in these microhabitats. The plant's rhizomes bind the silt and sand substrate into dense mats and draw nutrients from the rich compost of the estuary substrate. Among the maze of passageways created by the swaying blades, juvenile salmon, spawning herring, sticklebacks, sculpins, pipefish, tubesnouts and flounder find cover and food.

Historically, Puget Sound's eelgrass habitat has suffered because of fill and the construction of seawall. The margins of Elliott Bay once were lined with lush submerged meadows. Thin bands now persist only along Alki Beach and Magnolia Bluff. Elsewhere in the Sound, eelgrass beds survive as patchy communities along the shores of protected waterways and embayments. Notable stands near ferry routes occur along the Anacortes shore of the Guemes Channel, west of the Guemes ferry crossing; along the shores of Friday Harbor, on San Juan Island; along the south shore of Bainbridge Island between Restoration and Beans points (visible from the Bremerton ferry at the entrance to Rich Passage); at Southworth, both north and south of the ferry dock; and in the harbor shallows at Tahlequah, at Vashon Island's southern tip.

Wetlands

Wetlands are transitional lands between terrestrial and aquatic geographic features. They are usually defined by biological communities—particularly of plants—for which the main environmental influence is abundant water. Soils tend to be saturated; standing water can be present much of the time. Wetlands occur along rivers and streams, around lakes, ponds and bogs, and even in meadows where groundwater oozes to the surface permanently or at seasonal intervals. They also occur at the saltwater edge, where high tides flood the low plains of river deltas and surge into coastal sloughs and marshes.

Wetlands form prime habitat for many species of birds, mammals, reptiles, amphibians and insects; complex food relationships link all members of the wetland community. Along the shores of Puget Sound, several distinct types of wetland occur. The saltmarsh consists of a low bench just above normal high tide. Frequently flooded during winter tides, saltmarsh plants are adapted to survive the drying effects of salt crystal buildup on their tissues. Coastal sloughs are often backwater channels or former channels of rivers. Cattails, rushes and sedges line the water, noisy with blackbirds and the rushing sounds of the comings and goings of ducks.

Wetland losses in Puget Sound have been staggering. Perceived as swampy wastelands, many thousands of acres have been diked, drained and "reclaimed," mostly for agricultural purposes. Between 1880 and 1940, nearly 9,000 acres of the original 10,000 acres of estuarine wetlands of the Snohomish River were converted to farmland. After 1940, industrial development along the edge of the city of Everett began intruding onto filled wetlands of the Snohomish River delta. Wetland "reclaimed" a small amount of the agricultural lands between 1947 and 1970, when dikes were damaged by floods and not repaired.

The greatest losses of wetlands have occurred on the soggy deltas of the Puyallup and Duwamish rivers, in Tacoma and Seattle, respectively. Intense industrial development has altered both these sites. At the mouth of the Puyallup, about 1,900 acres of wetland was filled between 1880 and 1940. Today, 14 acres of marshland remain.

Built habitat

Bulkheads. As described in an earlier chapter, many segments of the Puget Sound shore have been modified to check erosion and protect upland property. The biological implications are significant. Generally speaking, seawalls create sediment-starved beaches because they increase the turbulence of breaking waves and accelerate the process of erosion. Increased wave energy also limits the variety in a community of organisms. In most cases, the higher the wave energy, the poorer—in species diversity and individual numbers—the living community. Since certain beaches on protected inlets serve as spawning grounds for surf smelt, seawall construction could inflict a loss of habitat that would threaten the reproductive success of a whole population.

Changing the slope of a shore also affects the behavior of prey species of fish, including juvenile salmon. The substitution of a deep-water shore (such as a sea-wall at high tide) for a gently sloping beach eliminates a band of shallow water into which migrating schools of small fish can retreat to avoid larger predators.

Although seawalls and rip-rap approximate some conditions found on a natural rocky shore, they rarely develop the rich communities of organisms found in the rocky intertidal zone. Because they often are isolated from communities that could "stock" the habitat, and built mostly above the intertidal zone, their ability to serve as substitute rocky intertidal habitat is severely limited.

Pilings, on the other hand, create remarkably complex habitat. In the intertidal zone, pilings often become festooned with bright green sheets of sea lettuce, delicate white sea anemones and packed communities of mussels and barnacles. Frequently, large seastars like the common ochre (often purple) seastar and the soft many-rayed sunflower star *Pycnopodia* are visible on the pilings around ferry slips. Distinctive bands of mussels and barnacles often are visible on pilings during low tides. These bands illustrate the effects of selective predation by seastars on mussels. Mussels survive in the upper ranges of the tide because they can withstand exposure to the air better than seastars. At lower tide levels where the seastars flourish, mussels are eaten, and therefore, absent.

Below the water, pilings create complex habitat for small fishes, especially the pile perch. Pile perch can reach about 16 inches in length, but are most often seen in schools of individuals not exceeding four or five inches. They feed on small mussels attached to the piles. Another subtidal organism found in pile habitats is the worm known as a featherduster worm or tubeworm. Tubeworms are segmented worms that grow to about 16 inches long, with their bodies enclosed in a thin hose of parchment-like substance. Protruding from the tube are gaudy plumes that retract suddenly when the animal is disturbed. Tubeworms themselves cluster tightly; a large colony creates microhabitat for a wide variety of other invertebrates.

Above the water, pilings serve as roosts (and sometimes nesting sites) for gulls and cormorants. The graceful profile of a cormorant drying its wings atop a distant piling is a sight familiar to even casual visitors on the waterfront. Other bird species utilize piling habitats: look for surf scoters—heavy black ducks with clown-paint faces—feeding in the turbulent water of the ferry slip.

Artificial reefs. As a way of enhancing recreational fishing in Puget Sound, numerous artificial reefs have been constructed. Early structures were composed of tires, belted together in bundles. More recent structures are composed of concrete rubble such as broken pipe, which remains more stable in areas of current and tidal action. The addition of irregular objects creates structural complexity, one of the key components of good habitat. Prey species find abundant hidey-holes that conceal them from predators. Predators' density increases with more prey, and with structures that create more available territories. Complex structural environments also attract a larger number of species.

Several artificial reefs have been constructed near the ferry dock at Edmonds, on what was formerly a broad expanse of sandy bottom. Fishermen and divers report increases in numbers and types of fish now utilizing the sites. Like natural banks, artificial reefs serve as orientation markers for migrating salmon. Salmon abundance can increase over a broad area in the vicinity of an artificial reef.

The habitat legacy

Even from a brief introduction of its constituent habitats, it is clear that Puget Sound possesses great variety in the conditions that support life. This is one of its most important legacies and will come to mean more for generations following our own. Because of limitations in the way humans can study the natural history of the marine environment, our knowledge remains in its infancy. As a fuller picture emerges of the interactions that characterize even relatively simple habitat-organism relationships, one truth stands above all others: the key to biological diversity is habitat diversity. Wildlife resources have become increasingly important in our society. We use them to monitor environmental health and they symbolize the quality of life we seek in the world where we live and spend our increasing leisure hours. But as human population increases, our need for food increases proportionately. And food—whether gleaned from the oceans or grown in the field—necessarily links us to the global biological process from which all "wild life" springs.

The marine world, resplendent with its myriad lifeforms, is a frontier of biological processes that awaits our attention. Its diversity and abundance will guide our own future as a species. Recognizing that the diversity and abundance of marine life are based on the quality of marine habitats is the first step toward protecting them—saving them for our necessary encounter with the future.

MARINE ORGANISMS

Food chains

Given Puget Sound's diversity of habitats, it isn't surprising that its lifeforms span a wide range of living organisms, from the simplest single-celled dinoflagellates swarming in the surface microlayer, to societies of orca whales, tracking returning salmon to the rivers. Wildlife occurs throughout Puget Sound, often in unexpected places. Industrialized waterfronts are home to great blue herons; glaucous-winged gulls nest on warehouse roofs. Suburban neighborhoods perched on blufftops include a few bald eagles as residents. Private docks become playgrounds for river otters. Always, the Sound teems with its common and exotic lifeforms.

Wildlife is one measure of environmental health. The presence or absence of wild animals is a measure of wildness in a place, of the balance between natural processes and the effects of changes we have brought to the ecosystem. In many ways, we measure our own quality of life by the robustness of Puget Sound's wild creatures. An abundance of salmon means satisfied sportfishers, enriched by the experience of catching the fish and sated by eating it. Tumor-ridden bottomfish warn us of toxic sediments dangerous to us.

There are many ways of understanding wildlife. One is to classify animals according to their genetic relationships, complex family trees, Latin names and physical characteristics. Unfortunately, such distinctions are often meaningful only to highly-trained specialists. They tell us little about the life-histories of the animals themselves and say much less about the environment in which the animals live or the functional link with us.

Perhaps the most direct connection that animals have among each other and, importantly, to the environment around them, is the process of eating. Certainly, this is one of the most tangible connections we have with the natural world. (Humans have yet to invent the food that isn't derived somehow from biological processes.) In this respect, the creatures of Puget Sound all are related to us. We are dependent upon the health of the fundamental food chains for our alder-smoked salmon and Dungeness crab salad. The processes that yield such delicacies are, in turn, dependent upon our stewardship of the common resource of Puget Sound—its water.

Marine food chains are the most productive of any known on earth. And, given the fact that about 71 percent of the earth's surface is covered by ocean, the sea makes an enormous contribution to life on our planet. This phenomenal productivity sustains intricate chains of living things, each connected, each necessary for the health of the whole community. The combined effects of sunlight, water temperature, the presence of nutrients and photosynthesis in marine algae drive this productivity cycle and support the tiniest organsims known, as well as the largest. Ultimately, this includes humans.

Although marine food chains ultimately have a primary energy source such as the sun (photosynthetic ecosystems) or deep ocean vents (chemosynthetic ecosystems), we can speak of two types of food chains at work in Puget Sound: the solar food chain and the detrital food chain (from *detritus*, or waste). The solar food chain is the easiest

to grasp because of its similarity to the major food chains of the land. On land and in the water, the major driving forces are sunlight and the process of photosynthesis.

In the marine environment, this process works only in the upper layers of the water column. Because it is fairly rich in nutrients and plankton, the water of Puget Sound is a poor conductor of light. Within the zone where sunlight is plentiful, it is converted in the cells of simple algae, kelp and submerged grasses into complex molecules of carbon, hydrogen and oxygen: simple sugar. This store of nutrients is passed from plants into plant eaters (herbivores); from plant eaters into meat eaters (carnivores); and frequently, from meat eaters into other meat eaters. Along each step of the way, energy from the sun is converted into body tissue or given off as heat or waste materials from the organism. At each step only about 10 percent of the total energy available in the organism is passed along to the next organism up the food chain. As a result, a phenomenal quantity of plant material (in marine environments, mostly phytoplankton) must be created to support populations further "up" the food chain.

A simple progression of steps could include the following: Filtering sunlight pours into a cloud of diatoms of the phytoplankton (*phyto*-plant; *plankton*-drifting). Sugar is formed in the tiny cells and the community "blooms." Larval crustaceans of the zooplankton *(zoo*-animal; *plankton*-drifting) feed on the diatoms. A shoal of herring encounters the tiny crustaceans, and feeds heavily by filtering zooplankton "soup" through their mouths and gills. They are the carnivores. An adult coho salmon seizes one of the herring. The salmon makes a pass at another herring, only to find itself caught on the hook of a cleverly contrived lookalike. This time the coho has fallen prey to a sportfisherman. Thus, sunlight falling on Puget Sound indirectly forms the dinner for a human instead of just a sunburn.

The detrital food chain is a recycling process, frequently occurring in the darkness of great depth. It also forms one of the ways that organic material entering Puget Sound through its rivers is incorporated into the marine food web. In a detrital food chain, scavengers forage on the decaying remains of once-living things. Such organisms may be filter feeders, like barnacles, which wave their legs rhythmically to strain out tiny bits of anything edible. They may be more like crabs, which roam the bottom, feeding opportunistically on protruding clam siphons or stripping putrid flesh from the carcass of a fish. Through the detrital food chain, organic material is continually passed on and eventually reduced to its mineral components. These settle into bottom sediments and lie trapped or they may be stirred into the water column by turbulence to fertilize the process anew.

The whole marine ecosystem demonstrates remarkable conservation in its complex and many-leveled system of food relationships. Very little is wasted—food scraps of one organism's lunch form another's dinner. Beginning with sunlight and minerals, organic substances are constructed into the complex tissues of living animals and plants, then recycled to their mineral components. This repeats endlessly. Puget Sound may represent only a tiny microcosm of the earth's marine system, but even in such a small world, the complexity and diversity which result are a wonder.

Invertebrates

Invertebrates are animals without backbones. In the marine environment, this broad group includes thousands of species that range in size and complexity from microscopic protozoa to giant squid. In all likelihood, you will see neither from the deck of a superferry heading across the Sound. But to understand Puget Sound as a biological entity, it helps to know what lies beneath the surface, so to speak, and to understand the processes that sustain the creatures we do see.

Jellyfish. The group of animals we call jellyfish belong to a phylum of invertebrates known as *Cnidaria* (pronounced "nide-AIR-ia"). Cnidarians possess powerful stinging cells to defend themselves and to stun their prey. Sea anemones are members of this phylum. Cnidarians are simple organisms that consist of two layers of specialized cells, one lining the digestive cavity, the other covering their exterior. Free-swimming cnidarians (as opposed to those attached to substrate) are referred to as medusas, because the mass of dangling tentacles resembles the serpent hair of the terrible character of Greek myth. In reality, each jellyfish (or medusa) is a colony of many individual polyps, some specialized as stinging cells, some specialized for reproduction and some specialized for feeding.

Puget Sound is blessed with many species of jellyfish. Most are between one quarter inch and two inches long and generally are present near the water surface during late summer. Larger types—those visible from ferries—come in two colors: clear and brown-orange. The most common clear jellyfish is the *Aurelia,* measuring between four and six inches in diameter. The largest jellyfish of Puget Sound is the *Cyanea,* which frequently attains a diameter of more than 20 inches. These jellyfish range in color from pale yellow to dull orange. Their tentacles can reach six feet in length and their sting is potent, though not lethal to humans.

Seastars are another group of invertebrates we occasionally glimpse from the ferry, but only as the boat is at or approaching the dock. Seastars belong to a large group of marine animals called Echinoderms, which refers to their spiny skin. Sea cucumbers, sea urchins and sand dollars also belong to this group.

Seastars range in their habitats from the lower intertidal zone to the deepest benthos of the aphotic zone. The most familiar is the tough, purple- or orange-colored ochre seastar common in many seashore habitats. Ochre seastars are often visible on pilings, rip-rap or bulkheads at low tide. Another seastar frequently seen near docks is the sunflower star *Pycnopodia.* This seastar has between 12 and 25 soft rays and sometimes reaches 30 inches in diameter. A voracious predator, *Pycnopodia* occasionally eats other seastars.

Octopus and squid

The **octopus** is a mollusc, generally related to clams and snails. Although this relationship may seem improbable, similarities include structures like the mantle and siphons. The eight arms of the octopus are actually a highly modified form of the "foot" found on snails and clams. Although shells are not present in local octopi, a tropical relative—the chambered nautilus—has a very elaborate shell.

Puget Sound hosts three species of octopus including the largest, *Octopus doflenei.* These carnivores inhabit nooks and crannies of the benthos, where they prey on crabs and fish. *Doflenei,* the Pacific giant octopus, occasionally reaches 20 feet in armspan and body weight of 120 pounds. Although they have been fictionalized as monsters, octopus are shy and retiring in nature. They display remarkable intelligence in captivity and possess the most sophisticated eye of any of the invertebrates, its structure paralleling that of humans. Puget Sound's other species of octopus are much smaller, rarely exceeding 12 inches in armspan.

Squid. You will not see octopus from the ferry. You may, however, witness great swarms of squid near the water surface during summer months, especially under bright lights at night at a ferry dock. Squid, like octopus, are molluscs. They have 10 arms rather than the eight of the octopus and what remains of their "shell" is a bony internal plate. Squid spend their time moving through the water, rather than settling into a cozy spot on the bottom. Seasonal migrations of squid bring them to Puget Sound in abundance. They shoot through the water in reverse, using their siphons and mantle for jet propulsion. They feed on small fishes, shrimp and other invertebrates. Squid of Puget Sound are mostly of two species *(Loligo opalescens* and *Gonatus fabricii)* and rarely exceed six inches in body length.

Bivalves

Clams are truly prodigious in Puget Sound. The "Old Settler's Song," popularized as "Acres of Clams" by the late Ivar Haglund, Seattle's best-loved bivalve restaurateur, lyricized the good fortune of the pioneer resigned to the fact that he is "surrounded by acres of clams." Indeed, as tidewater timber vanished around Puget Sound, clams became a new measure of abundance for the region.

As a year-round source of protein, clams long have figured into the subsistence patterns of Puget Sounders. The shift from terrestrial animals to the wealth of this intertidal resource marked a great transition in the prehistoric economy and culture. Clams could be collected in great quantities and preserved very easily by drying and smoking. The resulting clamshell heaps (known as shell middens) form the most extensive archaeological evidence that we have of pre-contact Native Americans.

Geoducks. The legendary geoduck ("goo-ey-duck") is the largest of the Puget Sound bivalves. These monsters attain a size of 12 inches and siphon length of up to 36 inches. Most intertidal geoducks have been harvested; subtidal geoduck beds are harvested by divers using a variety of suction and hydraulic dredges to remove them from the substrate. Geoducks can live as long as 75 years, and grow very slowly. Large populations of geoducks are present in the Sound.

Littlenecks. Puget Sound has two forms of littleneck clams, often called "steamers." These clams live on gravel beaches, taking advantage of porous pebble and cobble substrate common to many of our beaches. The native littleneck *(Protothaca staminea)* was once common throughout the Sound. Today, it is found only in small numbers over most of the Sound and in abundance only in the cold, clean water of Sequim and Discovery bays on the Strait of Juan de Fuca. This clam prefers a relatively low station on the beach—areas exposed by low tides. The Japanese littleneck or "Manila" clam resembles the native, and was introduced early in the century from the western Pacific. Manilas show greater tolerance for silty or less-pristine water and are found higher on the beach than the natives. Manilas are the dominant small hardshell clam of the Sound, occupying much of the former range of the native.

Butter clams *(Saxidomus giganteus)* are medium-sized hardshell clams that thrive on cobble beaches. Butters are distinguished by rough concentric ridges and whitish color. Also called "Washington" clams, butters are heavily favored for chowder.

The **horse clam** *(Tresus capax)* approaches the geoduck in size, but doesn't hold up as well as a delicacy. The horse clam lives closer to the surface than the geoduck, most often in silty, pebbly or cobble beach. Unlike the geoduck, the horse clam can retract its siphon almost entirely into its shell. Horse clams frequently host small commensal crabs commonly called "pea crabs" (see below).

Another clam found on Puget Sound beaches is the **heart cockle** *(Clinocardium nuttallii)*, with its conspicuous radiating ridges. Cockles seem to prefer finer substrate and often are seen in large numbers in the silt of eelgrass beds. Several species of soft-shell clams also live in the muddy bottom of estuaries. The **bentnose clam** *(Macoma nasuta)* reaches a length of about two inches and features a conspicuous bend in its shell. Its relative, *Macoma irus,* also lives in the mud of the quieter waters. Irus is heavier in appearance and lacks the kink of the shell.

Mussels are the most common bivalves seen from ferries. Large masses of them cling to pilings around ferry docks and can be seen at low tide. The band of mussels on a piling, visible at the lowest tides, is a spatial pattern created by two important restraining forces on mussel populations. The upper limit of the mussel colony is mainly determined by the highest point that mussels can survive being exposed to the air and sunlight. They can endure the frequent airing-out of normal tide cycles. Their lower limit is determined by the range of the Pisaster seastar, a voracious mussel predator. The seastars are more vulnerable to drying than the mussels and therefore stay lower on the piling. Thus, the distribution of a community of mussels on a piling is a band that represents an area of balance between drying out and being eaten. Two major species of mussel inhabit Puget Sound—the California mussel *(Mytilus californianus)* of the rocky, wave-washed intertidal zone, and the edible mussel *(Mytilus edulis)* of the quieter, more-protected waters. California mussels are more typical of the outer coast and are found in the inland waters only on the wave-lashed shores of the Strait of Juan de Fuca. Edible mussels, perfectly at home in more sluggish currents, are distributed throughout the rest of the Sound.

Mussels attach themselves to the substrate by means of tiny threadlike fibers called byssus. Masses cluster together, creating a porous surface that many other small organisms use as habitat. Mussels feed like other bivalves, by moving water in and out through siphons, gleaning suspended particles from the rich salty soup.

Tubeworms

The piling habitat that supports mussels also supports another form of marine life—the tubeworm. Tubeworms are segmented worms that occupy areas exposed only by the lowest tides and below. Several similar species are common in Puget Sound. Underwater, they take the appearance of feather dusters (they are often called "feather duster" tubeworms) as their lacy, plumelike gills strain the water for drifting debris. Tubeworms are more than mere occupants of the piling habitat—densely clustered together in groups, they *become* the habitat, adding to the structural complexity of the environment because the relatively tough tubes in which the worms live offer hiding places for small fishes and invertebrates and places to attach for yet other forms of marine life. Most Puget Sound public aquariums feature tubeworms among their displays; seeing these remarkable organisms up close lets you more fully appreciate their role in the subtidal marine community.

Crabs

Puget Sound crabs come in a wide variety of colors, shapes and sizes. he most popular, the Dungeness crab, is widely regarded as one of our most succulent seafoods. In their ecological role, however, Dungeness crabs are but one species of many that play an important role in the detrital food chain, breaking small bits of generalized organic debris into even smaller components. Other crabs of Puget Sound include the **rock crab,** also exploited for recreational and gastronomic purposes (though not in commercial quantities), and a host of smaller species that inhabit reefs, shores, eelgrass and kelp beds. By far the most spectacular of the Puget Sound crabs is the reclusive **Puget Sound king crab.** This crab often reaches more than 12 inches across its rough carapace (the shell on its back), which is mottled with brilliant orange, pink and purple colors. These king crabs (not to be confused with Alaska king crabs) have short, thick-shelled legs that fold neatly under the carapace, making them virtually indistinguishable from an algae-encrusted rock. They occupy deep water and are solitary animals.

Spindly little **kelp** and **decorator crabs** live among kelp beds. They often can be seen in free-floating rafts of kelp that have come unmoored and washed up on the beach. Decorator crabs received their name from the fact that they attach small bits of seaweed, sponge and other debris to their carapace, which aids in their concealment.

One species of crab often encountered by people unexpectedly is the **pea crab,** a parasite of mussels, horse clams, geoducks and other clams. Pea crabs spend their lives in the mantle cavity of bivalves, gleaning nutrients from the water that moves through the clam's body. Newcomers to Puget Sound seafood often register disgust at the thought of eating a parasite with their steamers. Seasoned palates, however, regard the tiny delicacy as a bonus—a crunchy crab garnish not listed on the menu, which elevates a mere plate of clams to the status of a full seafood platter.

It is the regal **Dungeness crab** that really makes mouths water. These purplish arthropods reach up to 8 inches across the carapace (only hard-shelled males over six inches are legal to keep) and are found in large congregations in areas of sandy bottom. Ferryboat naturalists occasionally see them from ferry piers above areas where the crabs roam along the sand. Dungeness crabs eat small clams (snipping off their siphons) and a wide variety of decomposing flesh. They tend to concentrate near stream mouths in shallow to moderately deep water and often are found at very low tide in eelgrass beds where they burrowed into the sand to weather the ebb. They are taken commercially, usually by boats with small power winches and davits along the sides of the work decks. Crab pots are marked with small floats.

Fishes

The areas near ferry docks and around piers and pilings form rich habitat for a group of fishes that thrive on bits of debris and small organisms associated with the piling community. Small, darting forms of the perches are often visible among the shadows beneath piers and alongside floats. Look also for sculpins, unsightly fishes frequently referred to as "bullheads."

Shiner perch *(Cymatogaster aggregata)* are the most common of these small fishes. Shiner perch are usually less than four inches in length, although some reach as much as seven inches. **Pile perch** *(Rhacochilus vacca)* are similar in appearance to shiners, except that they have broad, dark vertical stripes on the body and reach greater size (up to 17 inches in length). Pile perch are considered worthy prey for pier-side anglers who use light tackle, baited with shore crabs, tubeworms or clams. **Striped perch** *(E iotoca lateralis)* are also sought-for sport quarry. These perch are brightly colored with narrow horizontal bands along the flanks and frequently have a tinge of blue. They reach up to 15 inches in length.

The most common sculpin of the Puget Sound nearshore environment is the **staghorn sculpin** *(Leptocottus armatus)*. The staghorn sculpin is often seen cruising slowly among pilings. It is dark-green to gray-brown in color, easily seen from above, with a broad head and slender body. Anglers shun the staghorn and most other sculpins because of the paucity of meat, the sharp spines on their heads, their

docility when hooked and the fact that they are persistent bait thieves. Puget Sound hosts many other species of sculpin, most of which share the staghorn's reputation as undesirable. One species, the **cabezon** *(Scorpaenichthys marmoratus)*, reaches about 32 inches in length and is pursued both by sport and commercial fishermen.

Bottomfish. The term "bottomfish" refers generally to a group of fish whose feeding habits and physical characteristics let them prosper on the benthos. Of these, soles and flounders have the most obvious physical adaptations to sedentary lives on sand and mud bottoms. These fish are occasionally seen from piers over shallow sandy bottoms. The most common is the **starry flounder** *(Platichthys stellatus)*. Starry flounders are mottled grey, with distinctive bands of black in their fins and tail. Although they may attain a size of 36 inches, those most commonly seen are about the size of a dinner plate.

The largest of the Puget Sound flounders is the **Pacific halibut** *(Hippoglossus stenolepis)*. Halibut are common in Puget Sound and regarded by many to be our finest sportfish as well as our premier eating fish. The reason anglers like halibut is their size. Sport-caught specimens sometimes exceed six feet in length. Halibut are caught using heavy rods, reels and lines with a variety of jigs and baits including octopus, squid and herring. Halibut anglers can be seen on the Port Townsend-Keystone ferry in the spring and summer.

Commercial fisheries for halibut nearly wiped out the big fish early in the 20th century. Although most of the pressure was focused off the Strait of Juan de Fuca, commercial fishers worked the banks off Port Townsend and elsewhere in northern Puget Sound.

Another prized "bottom fish" is the **lingcod** *(Ophiodon elongatus)*. Actually not a cod at all, the lingcod is a voracious predator that reaches about five feet in maximum length. Many sportfishers prefer the ling to salmon because of its size, aggressive behavior and moist flesh. Like the halibut, lings live in deeper water on the banks. They are often caught on the same gear halibut fishers use. Intensely territorial, lingcod have suffered from overharvest by spearfishers. When guarding their egg masses, males are reluctant to flee and are easy prey. Strict seasons and limits have been imposed to protect them.

Herring. The **Pacific herring** *(Clupea harengus)* is an important commercial fishery resource as well as a critical component of the Puget Sound food web. Their name is thought to be derived from an old High German word, "herr," which means army or multitude. If that is the source of the name, it is appropriate. Great shoals of herring occur throughout Puget Sound.

Spawning occurs between mid-February and late March in most Sound locations. In the southern Strait of Georgia, herring spawn at Cherry Point in April and May. Spawning females carry as many as

38,000 eggs. Herring spawn in shallow water, usually in eelgrass beds. Eggs and milt are released into the water, sometimes clouding whole coves with the milky spawn. Eggs in great masses attach to eelgrass, kelp and other submerged objects. In Central Puget Sound, large flocks of grebes sometimes congregate on the spawning beds to feed on the tiny eggs. Undisturbed eggs hatch in about 10 to 14 days.

Upon hatching, the larvae are about one quarter inch in length and swim near the surface. By June, Puget Sound herring are seen near the surface toward evening, in Elliott Bay, Sinclair Inlet and other bays. By late summer, the juveniles are about four inches long and moving in very large schools. During August, September and October a common sight on Puget Sound is a sudden frenzy of feeding activity by gulls and other birds. This is usually associated with what is called a "herring ball." Herring balls are surface concentrations of juvenile herring reacting to the harassment of predators by forming dense balls. In effect, every fish in the school is trying to get to the center to avoid being eaten. A herring ball three to four feet in diameter may consist of as many as 10,000 fish. Herring balls are frequently preyed upon by gulls on the surface, and diving birds, dogfish, salmon and seals underwater. They are frequently observed off Restoration Point, on the Bremerton ferry route; near Kingston, on the Edmonds-Kingston route; off Port Townsend on the Keystone-Port Townsend route; and at many locations in the San Juans.

Another very unusual sight associated with herring predation occurs near Port Townsend: large schools of black rockfish abandon their normal kelp-bed habitat to follow shoals of herring into the open water. Observers report the surface teeming with the dull, blue-black fish as they feed on the shallow banks of silvery herring.

A commercial fishery for bait herring in Central Puget Sound yields about 600 tons per year. A herring roe fishery near Cherry Point yields between 100 and 1,000 tons per year when the Washington Department of Fisheries permits a harvest.

Salmon. Taken together, the Pacific salmon of the genus *Oncorhynchus* ("on-ko-RINK-us") are, by far, the most important fish resource of the Sound. Their prehistoric importance to Native Americans, their historic place in the natural resource economy of Washington State and their profound ecological role make them powerful symbols of the ecological and cultural web of the Pacific Northwest.

The largest of the salmon are the **Chinook** or **kings** *(Oncorynchus tshawytscha* ["cha-WEAT-sha"]). Chinook salmon spawn in the turbulent water of the largest rivers. Their spawning grounds are, typically, fast-moving reaches of water where the bottom is covered with fist-sized cobbles. The loss of river habitat has been felt most dramatically for Chinook; their preferred rivers are also those desirable for hydroelectric power production. Following emergence of the fry, Chinook leave the rivers quickly and begin their ocean odyssey which may last up to five years. Upon their return to Puget Sound they may weigh as much as 60 pounds. They typically move along the nearshore deep in the water, seeking shelter and food in kelp beds. Anglers fishing for Chinook "mooch," or let their bait descend to the bottom, where the hungry kings feed, alternately bringing the herring bait off the bottom and then letting it resettle.

A second type of Chinook that forms an important Puget Sound recreational fishery is the "blackmouth." **Blackmouth** are Chinook that either return to the Sound prematurely or leave the Sound late and spend a year in residence. These fish are smaller, and lack signs of sexual maturity.

Coho or **silver** (*O. kisutch*) **salmon** are second in importance to recreational and commercial fishermen. Coho prefer to spawn in slower water where the gravel is smaller. Following the emergence of the fry, coho spend as much as a year as river residents. Winter habitat such as beaver ponds and sloughs is critical for the juvenile fish, particularly when rivers are swollen with early spring freshets and the small fish seek refuge in side channels and tributary streams. During the summer, coho suffer from low water conditions where inadequate oxygen can be lethal. At all times of the year, coho require the shelter of logs, stumps and other woody debris in the streams—structural

diversity in the habitat that provides feeding territory for many of these solitary and competitive juveniles. Following their first year, coho move into the salt water. Several weeks are spent in the estuaries of the river mouths as they become acclimated to salt water. Here they grow quickly. Gradually, they move toward the open ocean and a two-year-long voyage that will carry them in a vast circle toward the northern Pacific and back. Upon their return, coho average about 10 to 15 pounds. They travel shallower in the Sound as they seek their natal rivers. Coho are most often taken by trolling herring and other lures or baits at relatively shallow depths.

Sockeye salmon (*O. nerka*) are among the most abundant of Pacific salmon, yet are not as common in the Puget Sound ecosystem as elsewhere in their range. Sockeye live in river systems with large lakes. Like other salmon, they spawn in rivers. Following emergence, the fry move into a lake, where they spend one or two years before migrating to the ocean. Once in the ocean, they spend one to three years feeding on plankton before returning to the rivers of their origin. Sockeye spawn in Lake Washington and Baker Lake, in the Skagit River system. Each summer, millions of sockeye stream through the San Juan Islands en route to the Fraser River system that drains British Columbia.

The **pink** or **humpbacked salmon** (*O. gorbuscha*) is unique in that it moves into saltwater at an earlier age than other Pacific salmon and spends precisely two years there. In Puget Sound, pinks return only in odd-numbered years. Because of their shorter ocean life-history phase, adult pinks return as smaller fish than other salmon. Because of their light, delicate flesh, pinks are attractive to commercial fishers and are caught mainly in the gill-net and purse seine fisheries. Puget Sound's major producers of pinks include the Stillaguamish, Skagit, Snohomish, Puyallup and Nooksack drainages. One run of pinks, in the Dungeness River of the Olympic Peninsula, spawns high in the steep watershed, unusual for this species. After emerging from the gravel, pink fry move quickly into the salt water. Once in Puget Sound, they school in shallows, apparently avoiding deeper water around piers, wharves and seawalls.

The **chum** or **dog salmon** (*O. keta*) is common throughout Puget Sound lowland and is seen early in the fall as it spawns in small streams near the Sound. The fish is called "dog" salmon because of its massive canine teeth that develop as the fish approaches spawning. These fish spawn in very shallow water and often are seen writhing up waterways too shallow to completely cover them. Characteristic are the purplish and brown streaks on their sides. Chum are fished commercially and canned. Their high oil content makes them good for smoking. Once they have returned to the rivers, however, the flesh of the fish is too soft for fresh consumption. Schools of chum fingerlings are sometimes seen from piers.

Trout. Two species of sea-running trout are found in Puget Sound—the steelhead and the cutthroat. Recent changes in the classification of Pacific salmon and trout have been made based on genetic studies of the fishes. Traditionally, steelhead and cutthroat were considered "true trouts," related to the Atlantic salmon and German brown trout. Fish experts now consider these fish more closely related to the Pacific salmon of the genus *Oncorhynchus.*

Steelhead are revered as the most noble of Washington river fish. Steelhead *(Oncorhynchus mykiss)* are races of rainbow trout that have taken a page out of the salmon life-history book by adopting a life cycle that takes them to sea. Life in the river is much like that of other rainbow trout until the juveniles move downstream and out into the estuaries and ocean.

The **cutthroat trout** *(Oncorhynchus clarki)* occurs throughout much of the Pacific Northwest and the western Rocky Mountains. In our coastal regions, anadromous, or sea-run, cutthroat move freely between streams and the marine waters. Saltwater trout fishing is popular during summer months when cutthroat roam the shallows in loose schools, preying on sand lance and other small fish. The fish return to their home-stream estuary in the late summer; as fall progresses, they enter the streams for spawning. Good sea-run habitat is common in Puget Sound. "Cuts" like small streams or the headwater reaches of larger streams for spawning. Young trout spend several years in their home streams before migrating to saltwater. Once in the Sound, they appear to stay near the home stream, cruising the nearshore currents along the beach.

Cutthroat may be visible from ferry docks over shallow bottoms. Most often, their presence is signalled by erratic surfacing behavior of schools of prey fish. Occasionally, cuts will jump out of the water while chasing their tiny prey.

Sharks and their relatives. Spiny **dogfish** (*Squalus acanthias),* the bane of most sport fishermen, are some of the most prolific predators in Puget Sound. According to one source, they are known to eat 27 species of fish and 13 species of invertebrates. Occasionally they are seen making quick turns near the surface of the water, particularly when large schools of herring or other forage fish are in the vicinity. These small sharks reach about four feet in length and have a prominent spine at the front of their second dorsal fin. Population structures of dogfish are of interest to fisheries biologists: this species is found in temperate waters of the northern hemisphere and some biologists believe that a similar southern hemisphere dogfish belongs to the same species. In spite of large dogfish populations in adjacent waters, Puget Sound spiny dogfish appear to mix very little with populations beyond the Admiralty Sill.

The **big skate** *(Raja binoculata)* occurs throughout Puget Sound, often in shallow enough water to be seen from a boat or from the beach or dock. Commonly mistaken as a "ray," the big skate moves with a fluid, flight-like motion of its oversized pectoral fins. Over sandy or gravel bottoms it is an impressive sight, as these fish often reach a size of five feet from "wingtip to wingtip." The big skate is easy to distinguish by its unusual shape and a prominent bull's-eye on each of its fins. Big skates are sought by some anglers for the meat of their large fins, described in flavor as similar to scallops.

Skates also are commonly seen in another puzzling form, that of their egg cases, which wash onto the beach following storms. The skate egg case is formed from leathery material enclosing a yolky egg. Baby skates live for months within the cases, consuming the protein of the yolk as they develop, and finally emerging as tiny adult-looking fish when the egg cases break up.

* * *

These are only a few of the forms of marine wildlife that make Puget Sound so varied and rich a biological resource. As impressive and diverse as the small group just described may be, they represent a tiny fraction of the lifeforms that hold the marine ecosystem together. Some of these organisms—mainly salmon and certain shellfish—support important commercial activity and strengthen the region's economy. Yet those economies are only as strong as the ecosystem that produces the resources. Many marine invertebrates and fishes have no obvious use or economic value. They may provoke our amazement when we encounter them. But they are certainly essential parts of the Puget Sound whole. We only skim the surface of Puget Sound in our knowledge and our experience of it. The living resources upon which we depend for economic benefit represent only the tip of a biological iceberg. That part unknown and unseen—underwater—is both the most vulnerable and the most important piece of the picture. Knowing this may be the key to the deepest appreciation of, and strongest protection for, Puget Sound.

MARINE BIRDS

Birds of Puget Sound are the most varied group of animals we regularly see. Puget Sound hosts migrating populations every season, and the cast of feathered characters shifts continuously as migrants wander in and out according to the timeless patterns that guide each species.

Feeding is perhaps the most observable and most easily understood of all animal behaviors. After all, it's something we ourselves do with great relish. Marine birds display an astounding variety of mechanisms for feeding which, in turn, helps explain the variety of appearance and habits we see. Indeed, like other organisms that have evolved from primarily land-dwelling animals, birds of the marine waters have adapted remarkably to the liquid medium of the marine environment—an environment in which they can neither live continuously nor reproduce.

Much of the anatomical and behavioral diversity among our seabirds stems from the problem of getting food. Some birds glean small organisms from the surface microlayer while others dive to considerable depth in pursuit of prey. Some wait motionless in shallow water for small fishes, then spring their head, spear-like, at the prey. Others have adopted strategies of piracy—harassing other birds into dropping food they have gathered. Among the behaviors the ferryboat naturalist sees displayed in Puget Sound marine birds, feeding patterns will help you recognize individual species and anticipate the presence of a given species based on other observable conditions.

Feeding strategies include wing-propelled underwater pursuit, foot-propelled underwater pursuit, plunging, surface feeding, surface feeding while flying, piracy and browsing.

Wing-propelled underwater pursuit is practiced by a group of seabirds known as "alcids." This family of seabirds includes rhinoceros auklets, tufted puffins, murres, murrelets and guillemots. These birds are small and blunt in appearance. The strength of their wings (needed for "flying underwater") is apparent in their flight through air—they fly with quick, forceful wingbeats, rarely gliding and never soaring. Captive alcids are part of the collections at Seattle and Pt. Defiance aquariums where their underwater pursuit tactics can be observed. Alcids feed primarily on small schooling fish like sand-lance and herring and are common throughout the Sound. Breeding populations occur mostly in the northern Sound, Strait of Juan de Fuca and San Juan Archipelago.

Foot-propelled underwater pursuit is practiced by a much larger group of seabirds, including the loons, grebes, diving ducks and cormorants. Like auklets and puffins, these birds pursue small fishes and can swim very quickly underwater. Some diving ducks feed on mussels and other bottom-dwellers as well. Loons and grebes have such well adapted feet and legs that they are practically useless on land. Many of these birds display adaptations that reduce their buoyancy. Loons, for example, are heavy and appear to float very low in the water; cormorants have feathers that absorb water, and spend considerable time drying their wings while perched on pilings or floating objects.

"Plunging" is a strategy seen in eagles, osprey, kingfishers, gulls and terns. These bird sight prey from the air and use the force of descent to carry them into the water, usually no deeper than their body lengths, where they seize prey in beak or claws. Terns and gulls that commonly fly alongside a moving ferry frequently display this feeding method.

Surface-feeding occurs commonly with birds that rest on the water's surface. Gulls are the most common scavengers of the surface, consuming floating bits of organic debris and small organisms swimming at the top of the water column. Tide rips are frequently very productive for scavenging—the vertical and horizontal mixing of convergence zones holds the debris along the boundary.

Surface-feeding while flying is another adaptation seen in this region, primarily in the storm petrels. These tiny "sea-sparrows" flit about the water surface feeding on tiny organisms and oil droplets while they appear to be dancing—their feet "pattering" the water surface. Storm petrels are rare in Puget Sound or the enclosed waters of the San Juan Islands. They are frequently seen, however, in the eastern Strait of Juan de Fuca, feeding among the debris rafts of the inner strait. Gulls occasionally feed at the sea surface while in flight as they "hover" facing into a strong wind.

Piracy is very common among gulls, who frequently "squabble" over food bits. Eagles are also known to steal, from osprey or other eagles. Acts of avian piracy are worth watching closely, because they are sometimes clues to the presence of the parasitic jaeger, a rare bird visitor that uses theft as its primary means of subsistence.

Browsing is a very general behavior used by a wide variety of waterfowl, shore and terrestrial birds. Gulls and crows forage the beach for scraps of washed-up organic material; sandpipers and other shore-birds forage for certain specific organisms.

Gulls

Probably the most common birds we encounter on the ferries are gulls. Gulls also provoke some of the most heated field identification disagreements among advanced birders. (I advise keeping quiet while veterans debate, with one exception: when the argument centers around glaucous-winged vs. western gulls, a greenhorn can sagely mediate by suggesting that the bird in question is, in all probability, a hybrid. Result: instant peer status.) Although most gulls are similar in appearance, beginners can distinguish some species based on their distinctive physical characteristics. The following accounts include only the most prominent or easily-identified Puget Sound gulls. Consult one of the field identification guides listed in the reference section for complete field marks for all the species (good luck!).

The most common Puget Sound gull is the *glaucous-winged gull (Larus glaucescens)*. Populations breed at many sites around the Sound, including many of the San Juan islands, Protection and Smith islands, and the Seattle and Olympia waterfronts. Glaucous-winged gulls are large gulls with bright white wings. They feed omnivorously, scavenging and preying on a wide variety of marine organisms, including herring and clams. They also prey on young birds of other species and frequently employ piracy as a feeding tactic. Glaucous-winged gulls demonstrate remarkable ingenuity in their methods of opening clams and other molluscs—they drop the shelled animals onto pavement or beach cobble to shatter the shells. They have benefited profoundly from human presence—they are frequently seen in cultivated fields and lawns feeding on worms driven to the surface by rain saturation, and they are present in hordes at landfill sites. Glaucous-winged gulls hybridize with western gulls *(Larus occidentalis)* where their breeding ranges overlap on the outer Washington coast. Estimates for Washington glaucous-winged gulls place the population at about 28,000-30,000 birds.

Heermann's gull *(Larus heermanni)* has a distinctive slate-blue body and red bill. These gulls breed off the coast of Mexico and visit Puget Sound during the summer to feed on marine organisms. Heermann's gulls are commonly seen in the San Juan Islands and on the Port Townsend-Keystone ferry route. In Admiralty Inlet, they mix with large flocks of glaucous-winged gulls and eagerly partake of feeding frenzies on herring balls (the spheres that threatened herrings form to protect themselves). They too are occasional pirates—one account states that they have been observed parasitizing parasitic jaegers.

Bonaparte's gull *(Larus philadelphia)* is a small gull recognized by its black head. These birds feed primarily on the surface, seizing fish and small marine organisms. They have been observed "pattering" like storm petrels, and gather in great flocks throughout northern Puget Sound. Look for jaegers among large flocks of Bonaparte's gulls.

Terns

Three species of terns are common visitors to Puget Sound. These birds are gull-like in some of their habits but easily distinguished by their sharply-pointed wings, flat, dark-capped heads, forked tails and floating motion in flight. Terns arrive in Puget Sound during the summer months and feed mainly on small fish. The **common tern** *(Sterna hirundo)* is the most numerous—large flocks are seen late in the summer in the San Juan Islands and in lesser concentrations elsewhere throughout Puget Sound. The **Caspian tern** *(Sterna caspia)* also visits Puget Sound. The **arctic tern** *(Sterna paradisaea)* presents an interesting anomaly—although other breeding populations occur hundreds of miles to the north, a small group established a breeding site on Jetty Island on the Everett waterfront in the late 1970s. This site is apparently no longer in use.

Terns generally feed by plunging. They scout the water below as they fly, fall rapidly when prey is sighted, and submerge themselves in their plunge. Terns are commonly harassed by jaegers.

Jaegers

The **parasitic jaeger** *(Stercorarius parasiticus)* gets its name from its nasty habit of piracy. Parasitic jaegers move into northern Puget Sound in July, closely following the migratory patterns of those species they most commonly steal from. Jaegers can be seen in the Strait of

Juan de Fuca, the San Juan Islands, Admiralty Inlet, Saratoga Passage and Possession Sound. An encounter with a jaeger is dramatic. Ordinarily, you will see what appears to be the normal squabbling for food among gulls and terns. The jaeger makes its appearance quickly, diving on individual birds and trying to force them to disgorge and drop morsels they have captured. As the harried bird drops its food, the jaeger plunges after it. The commotion raised in a flock of gulls or terns by a jaeger is often the first sign that something is awry. Look for a dark gull-like bird with pointed wings, a dark cap on its head and central tail feathers extending beyond tail feathers on either side. Two other species of jaeger visit northern Puget Sound on rare occasions. The **Pomarine jaeger** *(Stercorarius pomarinus)* and **long-tailed jaeger** *(Stercorarius longicaudus)* remain farther off Washington's coast, occasionally wandering into our inland marine waters.

Shearwaters and storm petrels

Both shearwaters and storm petrels are oceanic by preference, wanderers of the landless horizon that use isolated islets and rocks only for nesting purposes. Shearwaters are seldom seen on the inside marine waters of Puget Sound. **Sooty shearwaters** *(Puffinus griseus)* are occasionally seen in the Strait of Juan de Fuca. Ferryboat naturalists should watch for long-winged dark birds soaring along wave crests with one wingtip almost touching the water. The grace of these birds is poetic—in a flight adapted to energy conservation over the vast ocean, these birds have mastered the microcurrent of air lifted by moving water. Relatively common off Tatoosh Island at the entrance to the Strait, they come inland only when blown by storm or disoriented by seafog. Watching for shearwaters on the Port Angeles-Victoria ferry run is a quiet pleasure that requires foul weather and tight foulweather raingear.

Leach's storm petrels *(Oceanodroma leucorhoa)* and **fork-tailed storm petrels** *(O. furcata)* are small birds sometimes called "sea swallows" by mariners. These birds flutter over the water surface, skittering unpredictably along the wave crests. Both are occasionally visible in the eastern Strait of Juan de Fuca as ferries from Port Angeles or Seattle ply the broad swells enroute to or from Victoria. These birds feed by "pattering," hovering just above the water, pecking small bits of fish eggs, zooplankton and organic debris from the sea-surface microlayer. Leach's storm petrels are dark in color, with white rumps; fork-tailed storm petrels are grey. Both are about the size of robins except for their slightly longer wings. In the eastern Strait of Juan de Fuca, look for them among the wind- and current-rows of floating debris in convergence zones.

Ducks and geese

For the naturalist intimate with the cycles of season, the sight and sound of distant strands of ducks or geese wheeling through the sky provoke inner conversations about the progress of the year. Unfinished tasks are remembered as winter draws near; new beginnings of spring are noted with irrepressible enthusiasm. Keeping track of these migrants forms a calendar of its own. Days spent on the water, marsh or stubblefield carry you through the rotation of months—the biting cold of oldsquaw January; the summer blush of mallard ducklings; the lengthening days of the gathering black brant. Puget Sound is blessed with annual migrations of a host of moving waterfowl. Many grace our region only in passing. Others linger through the winter, gathering into great flocks that darken the water's edge or pierce the gray light of winter with flecks of white. Like other marine birds, ducks, geese and swans can be divided roughly by feeding strategies. These strategies also help us place the birds in their respective habitats.

Many ducks and geese prefer the freshwater environment to the saltchuck. **Mallards** *(Anas platyrhynchos)*, **pintails** *(Anas acuta)*, **green-** and **blue-winged teals** *(Anas crecca* and *A. discors*, respectively) are all primarily vegetarians, although each eats small crustaceans and molluscs. On Puget Sound, these ducks are seen along estuary shores and in adjacent wetlands.

Puget Sound geese include the Canada goose *(Branta canadensis)*, white-fronted goose *(Anser albifrons)*, black brant *(Branta bericla)* and snow goose *(Chen caerulescens)*. These birds forage the shores and shallows of our estuaries, eating mainly vegetable material including sea lettuce *(Ulva)*, eelgrass and other wetlands vegetation. **Canada geese** are very common—certain resident populations nest in freshwater wetlands throughout the Puget Lowland. Most Canada geese and all of the other goose species are migrants for whom Puget Sound's estuaries are critical stopover points on their long migrations.

White-fronted geese are large, grey geese seen in spring and fall, feeding on eelgrass beds of Dungeness and Skagit bays. **Black brant** are small sea geese that traditionally gather on tide flats throughout Puget Sound to feed mainly on eelgrass. The loss of eelgrass beds all along the Pacific coast has had a devastating impact on brant. Wetland losses in great estuaries including Mission Bay (San Diego) and San Francisco Bay in California and in Grays Harbor, Washington have caused brant numbers to decline. Major Puget Sound staging areas for the flocks include Padilla, Skagit and Dungeness bays, the Great Bend of Hood Canal, open waters of the eastern Strait of Juan de Fuca, and the Nisqually River delta. Look for brant during spring and fall in small numbers at river mouths and other places where eelgrass grows and the birds have plenty of open space in which to observe predators. **Snow**

geese migrate through Puget Sound and some populations spend the winter here, concentrated in the coastal areas of northern Puget Sound. Look for wintering snow geese in Skagit and Port Susan bays and near the Stillaguamish River delta.

Among the ducks, shallow-water feeders include **American widgeon** *(Anas americana)*, **northern shoveler** *(Anas clypeata)*, **lesser** and **greater scaup** *(Aythya affinis* and *A. marila*, respectively), **Barrow's** and **common goldeneye** *(Bucephala islandica* and *B. clangula*, respectively*)*. These birds are seen during the winter along the edges of many of our bays and estuaries.

The so-called diving ducks inhabit deeper waters of bays and estuaries. When these birds dive, they propel themselves with their feet to feed on small molluscs and crustaceans. This group of ducks represents some of our most common and widely dispersed winter visitors and includes oldsquaw *(Clanula hyemalis)*, bufflehead *(Bucephala albeola)*, white-winged, common and surf scoters *(Melanitta fusca, M. nigra* and *M. perspicillata*, respectively) and harlequin duck (*Histrionicus histrionicus*).

The **oldsquaw** is the most timid of the group and arguably the most beautiful. Males and females are white with dark wings. Males possess long, trailing tails that whip conspicuously when the birds dive. Males in winter plumage have soft magenta cheek patches. The song of

the oldsquaw rivals that of the loon—winter stillness broken by the melodious yodel is a delightful surprise. These birds often stay well offshore. Stay alert for them as the ferry moves into the channel or approaches the shore.

The **bufflehead** is a small duck bedecked with brightly contrasting black and white plumage. Look for them in most bays and inlets. Males have a large white patch on the head; females are distinguished from goldeneyes by the small white patch just behind the eye (in goldeneyes, the white spot is in front of the eye).

Scoters are common winter residents, seen in harbors and near pilings, where they feed on mussels. Scoters often raft up into large flocks, and males are distinguished from other ducks by their ungainly and decorative bills. On the surf scoter, this oversized schnoz is brightly colored with orange, black and white; common and white-winged scoters have a bulbous protuberance perched atop the bill. White-winged scoters, true to the name, have obvious white patches on the wings. Female scoters are sometimes confused with other dark ducks; they're the ones that seem to stay close to their bozo male companions.

Harlequin ducks are small blue-grey sea ducks that frequent rocky shores. Males have a distinctive plumage pattern of white spots, mixed with rust and black. Harlequins are visible during the winter in small concentrations offshore; during the summer, they move into the rivers for breeding. Males often gather on remote beaches in great congregations during June to undergo a flightless molt. Densely packed together, they resemble the cobble beach itself.

Diving birds

The diving birds represent a very close fit between birds and the marine environment. Among them, we see a powerful and startling adaptation of flight—its use underwater, in a medium hundreds of times more dense than the air in which feathers, bones and muscles of the bird wing evolved. Underwater flight allows the birds that use it to move with great speed in pursuit of their quarry. In Puget Sound seabirds, this method of underwater propulsion is used by rhinoceros auklets, tufted puffins and their relatives of the family *Alcidae,* collectively known as "alcids."

The **rhinoceros auklet** *(Cerorhinca monocerata)* gets its name from a yellow, rhinoceros-like horn on its beak. These compact birds fly through the water pursuing herring, sand-lance smelt and other small fishes of the Sound. During summer months, "rhinos" nest in abundance on Protection and Smith islands. Daily, these breeding birds scatter to Admiralty Inlet, throughout the San Juans and other reaches of the northern sound. Summer evenings at Protection Island are busy times as flights of the birds return to their island nests. Their powerful wingbeats move them quickly, low across the water. Wintering populations of rhinoceros auklets are found in South Puget Sound. Researchers are uncertain whether these birds are of the summer breeding population.

The **tufted puffin** *(Lunda cirrhata)* also pursues its underwater prey using its wings for propulsion. These birds are common in only a few localities in the San Juans and Admiralty Inlet. Like the rhinoceros auklets, they nest on islands, where their burrowing habit makes them vulnerable to mammal predators. Historically, puffins nested in greater abundance than now; loss of nesting habitat is certainly the cause. Puffins are the clowns of the summer seabird population. Their bills seem oversized and they possess bright tufts of feathers over their eyes. The combination of a huge, colored beak and bushy "eyebrows" make them easy to identify. Look for these birds in Rosario Strait, Admiralty Inlet, Haro Strait and the eastern Strait of Juan de Fuca feeding on small fishes in deep water.

Three other closely-related species of diving seabirds occur in Puget Sound and can easily be seen by casual observers. Like the auklet and puffin, these are members of the alcid family. The **marbled murrelet** *(Brachyramphus marmoratus)* is a small, diving bird with a puzzling life-history. Although fairly common in Rosario Strait, the Strait of Juan de Fuca and through the San Juan Islands during its summer breeding season, no nest has ever been found in Washington and it is thought that this bird nests far inland in old-growth forests. Concern is mounting for these birds. While we may not know exactly where they nest, we do know that old-growth forests are vanishing at an alarming rate. Because of the loss of this forest habitat, we may learn of the birds' dependence on old growth only after we have destroyed its breeding places.

The other threat to marbled murrelets comes from the marine environment in which it feeds. Marbled murrelets are among many species of seabird that suffer high mortality because of the use of nets for fishing, particularly the gill-net fishery. With no formal reporting mechanism required of fishermen who have an "incidental take" of the birds, researchers don't know how the population is being affected. These small seabirds easily escape notice because of their preference for open-water feeding sites and their obscure breeding behavior. Unless we learn a great deal about them soon, their obscurity in Puget Sound may become permanent.

The **pigeon guillemot** *(Cepphus columba)* is a common diving bird throughout Puget Sound. Breeding populations are found on many beaches and soft bluffs. This bird is about the size of a common pigeon. During the summer, they are black with white patches on the wings. A conspicuous identifying mark is their red feet, seen as they run over the water on take-off. Guillemots are easily disturbed on their nest sites, which frequently are among drift logs on beaches. A single curious dog with a good nose can disrupt many brooding birds. Guillemots feed, like other alcids, on small fishes taken while diving in pursuit.

The most common diving bird of the alcid family, and Washington's most abundant breeding seabird, is the **common murre** *(Uria aalge)*. Murres vaguely resemble penguins (although they are no more closely related than other alcids) and inhabit the open waters of Northern Puget Sound and the Strait of Juan de Fuca. Large flocks of murres often are disrupted by the ferryboat that crosses between Port Townsend and Keystone. Look for murres among convergence zones, where they prey upon forage fish including sand lance and herring.

The cormorant, its wings half-spread atop a piling, is one of Puget Sound's most common wildlife sights. Wing-spreading is also a clue to one adaptation that helps this diving bird feed—its feathers are wettable and help the bird reduce buoyancy in order to dive deeply to feed. Draping its wings maximizes the bird's ability to dry its plumage. Cormorants are some of our deepest divers, capable of plucking bottomfish from as deep as 150 feet. Cormorants dive without the aid of their wings; they are endowed with heavy webs between their toes that facilitate their powerful underwater movement.

Cormorants in Puget Sound are members of three species: pelagic cormorant *(Phalacrocorax pelagicus)*, Brandt's cormorant *(P. penicillatus)* and double-crested cormorant *(P. auritus)*. **Pelagic cormorants** breed in many sites in Northern Puget Sound. This bird is the smallest of the three species and distinguished during the summer breeding season by white flank patches, visible as the birds lift off the water and fly away. Its slender neck and narrow tail distinguish it at other times of the year. **Brandt's** and **double-crested cormorants** are very similar in field marks and relatively hard to distinguish at a distance. One difference is that double-crested cormorants have more prominent bends in their stocky necks. Up close (such as on a piling along the ferry dock), look for a bluish pouch beneath the bill of the Brandt's—double-crested cormorants have a dull orange pouch. Double-crested cormorants nest at many sites in Northern Puget Sound and the San Juans. Most Brandt's cormorants in Puget Sound are winter visitors.

Grebes form a group of Puget Sound deep divers that commonly winter here, often gathering in great flocks that work stretches of water in concert, diving and rising together. (On one occasion in Budd Inlet, I saw several hundred western grebes on the water's surface. A moment later, they had vanished. Curious, I watched for several minutes and saw the mass of them bob up at about the same time.)

Four species of grebe are commonly seen: western grebe *(Aechmophorus occidentalis)*, red-necked grebe *(Podiceps grisegena)*, horned grebe *(P. auritus)* and eared grebe *(P. nigricollis)*. Grebes are wonderfully adapted to speedy underwater pursuit of prey—their legs are placed far back on their bodies and their feet consist of separate toes, each shaped like a fleshy canoe paddle as they kick.

Western grebes are the largest and can be identified by their white necks and long, sharp, bright yellow bills, which they use to spear and seize their prey, a variety of small fish, molluscs and crustaceans. Western grebes are common winter and spring visitors often seen feeding around piers and ferry terminals throughout Puget Sound. **Red-necked grebes** are only slightly smaller than western grebes. They are frequently confused with westerns because of their similar size and the fact that during winter months, their necks are not really red—that's the breeding plumage they save for the marshes of the interior West. In winter plumage, their necks are dull grey, contrasted with the white of their larger cousins. Red-necked grebes were particulary hard-hit in the 1985 *ARCO Anchorage* oil spill at Port Angeles. Nearly 1,000 birds of this species were oiled, and almost all died. Their greatest concentration was a great convergence zone just off Dungeness Spit, where the birds were apparently feeding when overtaken by the slick of crude oil. An interesting footnote about the red-necks is that the number killed was greater than the number previously estimated to inhabit the region. The spill and its outcome demon-

strated how little we really know about the seasonal abundance of these and other animals.

Eared and **horned grebes** are smaller and less often seen in large flocks. The birds are fairly similar in appearance during the winter. Horned grebes are common in Puget Sound, eared grebes uncommon. Horned grebes display a white neck during the winter; eared grebes have a grey neck. Horned grebes remain in Puget Sound long enough to develop breeding plumage. As springtime deepens, the birds develop brilliant rust-colored necks and flashy swept-back feathers that form the avian equivalent of a punk hairdo.

Loons are large, heavy birds that visit Puget Sound during the winter months to feed. Four species occur here: the common loon *(Gavia immer)*, the Pacific loon *(G. pacifica)*, the red-throated loon *(G. stellata)* and the yellow-billed loon *(G. adamsii)*. While diving, these birds benefit from their heavy builds and weighty bones, which help them overcome buoyancy. Their heaviness is apparent in the way they float on the surface—very low in the water—and in their distinctive flight profiles: outstretched neck sagging slightly lower than the bodies. The **common loon** frequents shallow to moderately deep and open water singly or in pairs, feeding on a wide variety of fishes and invertebrates. The **Pacific loon** is slightly smaller and frequents the rough water of tide rips and surging currents in passes and eddies. Look for this bird throughout Puget Sound in large flocks in deeper and more turbulent water. Each winter the San Juan Islands host North America's largest concentration of loons—great rafts of Pacific loons feed in the current convergences of the islets. **Red-throated** and **yellow-billed loons** are much more at home closer to shore and are seen along estuary edges feeding on small fishes and invertebrates.

Birds of prey

The first clue to the presence of the **belted kingfisher** *(Megaceryle alcyon)* is its rattle-like call. Look for its erratic, dipping flight and follow it to a perching place on a piling, telephone wire or madrona bough. Kingfishers are small birds with heads that look oversized on their bodies. These sharp-eyed birds seek their prey from the air, plunging violently when they dive.

The stately soaring motion of the **bald eagle** *(Haliaeetus leucocephalus)* is an auspicious sight. This bird, our national symbol, flies with wings outspread like a plank, primary feathers bending slightly at the wingtips. Easily distinguished as adults by the unmistakable white head and tailfeathers, these birds are frequently sighted perching upon the gnarled limbs of shore trees. The bald eagle earns its living two ways. As a majestic predator whose fishing prowess is awesome when observed in action, the bird can lift adult samon from the water. Its other livelihood is as a scavenger, not-so-heroically quarreling with crows and gulls over the softening remains of once-living beach debris. Eagles are common throughout Puget Sound; make a practice of scanning the dark forest horizon for this unmistakable—and unforgettably spectacular—bird of prey.

The **osprey** *(Pandion haliaetus)* is less common in the marine environment than farther inland, yet occasionally appears on Puget Sound. This bird was particularly hard-hit by pesticides. Its breeding success was drastically hampered by eggshell-thinning DDT. Osprey are fishhawks, depending entirely on fish and small amphibians for their subsistence. Look for a lanky, light-colored hawk with gull-like "kinks" in its wings. Osprey have been seen fully submerging themselves as they dive for fish. Occasionally, they hover high over the water before they begin their freefall pursuit dive.

The **peregrine falcon** *(Falco peregrinus)* also suffered badly from pesticides and today is listed as endangered on both federal and state species lists. Peregrines are frequently associated with the marine environment—their principal prey include shorebirds, ducks, seabirds and pigeons. The fury of a peregrine kill is breathtaking. Falcons strike at blinding speed, often seizing their quarry mid-air in an explosion of feathers. Peregrines migrate with populations of their prey. In Puget Sound, look for peregrines at major estuaries and near seabird nesting colonies.

The **gyrfalcon** *(Falco rusticolus)* is an uncommon falcon of the northern shores of Puget Sound. This powerful predator is larger than the peregrine in size, although slower in its dive. The gyr breeds in the Arctic and visits this region only during the winter. Infrequent sightings have been near Bellingham.

The **northern harrier** or marsh hawk *(Circus cyaneus)* is a common predator of fields and marshes adjacent to Puget Sound. This hawk is slender and carries a distinctive white patch on its rump. Males are gray and smaller than the brown females. The harrier gets its name from its habit of hovering over its prey: small rodents, frogs, fish and birds.

Shorebirds

The **black oystercatcher** *(Haematopus bachmani)* inhabits rocky shores. This bird is jet black, with a bright red bill. Contrary to the name, oystercatchers do not eat oysters. Its principal prey items are mussels. Using their stout bills, oystercatchers pry open the musselshell just far enough to admit the bill and then snip away the muscle that holds the shell closed. Oystercatchers are considered indicators of high-quality rocky intertidal shore—look for them along remote sections of shorelines at the tideline. When disturbed, oystercatchers fly over the water raising a loud peeping call.

The shorebirds of Puget Sound form a large and varied group. Space here precludes discussion of the group in any but the most general terms. For positive field identification marks and notes on life-histories, check with bird field guides listed in the reference section.

Shorebirds are generally divided into three groups: plovers, sandpipers and phalaropes.

Plovers are small birds with short, stubby bills. They nest on beaches and mudflats. The most common plovers include the **killdeer** *(Charadrius vociferus)*, a shorebird that has moved inland and now is common on flat roofs and fields many miles from water. Our common shore plovers include the **black-bellied plover** *(Pluvialis squatarola)*, the **semipalmated plover** *(Charadrius semipalmatus)* and the **American golden plover** *(Pluvialis dominica)*.

Sandpipers comprise a large group of birds with long, slender beaks adapted to probing the sand for small invertebrates. In all, 31 species of sandpiper occur in the Pacific Northwest. Along Puget Sound shores sandpipers fitting every possible combination of beak-length and leg-length are present. Ideally, this differentiation enables each species to exploit a unique food source. In reality, species may overlap in their prey selection. Small sandpipers with short legs and beaks inhabit the beach, drilling into the sand or mud for small invertebrates. Larger birds with longer legs wade. Birds with longer beaks probe deeper into the sand or mud.

The most common small sandpipers are **dunlins** *(Calidris alpina)*, **least sandpiper** *(Calidris minutilla)*, **western sandpiper** *(Calidris mauri)*, and **sanderling** *(Calidris alba)*. Larger sandpipers include the **whimbrel** *(Numenius phaeopus)*, **greater yellowlegs** *(Tringa melanoleuca)* and **long-billed dowitcher** *(Limnodromus scolopaceus)*.

Phalaropes are occasionally referred to as swimming sandpipers because they are frequently seen at great distances from shore. Look for phalaropes among the San Juan Islands, where they feed in the passages and tidal currents on tiny invertebrates caught at the surface in the convergence zones. Phalaropes demonstrate an unusual surface feeding behavior by swimming rapidly and erratically in circles. This apparently moves their small prey to the surface where their sandpiper-like beaks can snatch the morsels. The **Northern phalarope** *(Phalaropus lobatus)* is the most common of the three species that occur here. **Wilson's phalarope** *(Phalaropus tricolor)* and the **red phalarope** *(Phalaropus fulcaria)* are rarely seen, mostly in the northern reaches of the Sound and among the San Juan Islands.

Although not classed as a shorebird, the **great blue heron** *(Ardea herodias)* is perhaps the most commonly seen wading bird associated with the shoreline environment. Great blues are conspicuous with their honking calls, and present wherever there is shallow water and their favored prey. Look for herons in quiet water along estuary margins, where they hunt for small fishes, amphibians and occasionally other animals including mammals. These majestic birds move stealthily in the shallows and stand motionless as they watch for their quarry. In a flash, the snakelike neck springs and the bird grabs or impales its prey with its long, pointed beak. Herons frequently gather in loose groups to hunt; six or eight are a common sight on a tideflat. Breeding herons gather into large congregations that return to the same nest site every year. Heron rookeries are located high in trees along rivers or wetlands. Dozens of large, ungainly nests may be found in a single grove of trees. Because they are so conspicuous, heron rookeries are vulnerable to disturbance. Fortunately, their human neighbors usually view heron rookeries as valuable assets and protect them as the law requires.

The importance of birds in the Puget Sound environment is easiest to prove by simply listening. Against the constant rush of waves or the steady hiss of a breeze are the punctuating cries, near and distant, of birds. Often, they are gulls. And when you really start listening, the other voices are heard. A scattering of shorebirds explodes in sight and sound on the shore. A gruff whimbrel takes flight and whistles. Somewhere under the dark, overhanging fir trees, a kingfisher chatters.

Puget Sound's birds are our most diverse and constant companions on and near the water. Like us, they must breed and breathe out of the water, gathering from the marine environment those things that live at its edge, in its shallows or upon its surface film. Yet, unlike us, marine birds demonstrate millions of years of adapting to the water world. They represent an odd assortment of body parts, fitted together in many ways, each of which

represents a successful natural strategy for gleaning food from the earth's most productive environment. And while they are delightful in and of themselves, Puget Sound's seabirds can teach us much about the Sound itself. It is they who signal the rising of a school of herring; it is they who betray the living multitudes buried in the beach sand. For the ferryboat naturalist, seeing and knowing Puget Sound birdlife is another key to experiencing and understanding the otherwise unseen and unseeable mysteries of the Sound itself.

MARINE MAMMALS

During the 1970s, two related trends led to the heightened awareness of marine mammals. One of these was the popularization of findings that marine mammals, particularly whales, possessed keen intelligence and complex social organization. The second was that many of these animals, even whole species, appeared on the brink of extinction because of outright harvest for meat, oil and other products and, more insidiously, from inadvertent impacts of pollution, habitat loss, physical disturbance and unwarranted hostility. World-wide, the campaign to save marine mammals gave the environmental movement a focus on a single group of visible and gravely endangered animals. Whales poignantly symbolized the sea and nature; the world ocean symbolized the earth itself. Around the world, activists devised strategies to stop whaling and ocean pollution.

Some strategies were conventional: laws, regulations and treaties. Others were some of the most controversial actions ever seen in environmental advocacy—the "direct action" of groups like Greenpeace, heroic to some, akin to piracy to others. That the campaign to preserve marine mammals assumed global dimension and such a wide divergence of tactics and opinion suggests that concern for marine mammals and the natural integrity of the marine environment had struck a resonant chord among many people. Both traditional laws and non-traditional tactics played important roles in the marine waters of the Pacific Northwest. In 1972, the Marine Mammal Protection Act was sponsored by the late U.S. Senator Warren G. Magnuson, and passed by Congress. Later, Magnuson sponsored an amendment to the act, forbidding the entry of supertankers into Puget Sound. The law still is controversial and now that some populations of marine mammals have retreated from the brink of extinction and show signs of vigor, calls for its repeal are becoming louder.

The other approach, direct action, also had its roots here in the Pacific Northwest. Greenpeace, now one of the largest environmental organizations in the world, was founded in Vancouver, B.C., where organizers saw local issues of whales and whale capture connected directly to ecological issues of the whole planet. Regardless of personal preference for methods to conserve marine mammals, any probability that you can observe these creatures from a Puget Sound ferry comes from a legacy, born and nurtured in this region, of love, concern and dedication to the marine world and its stateliest inhabitants.

Marine mammals in Puget Sound are divided into three groups—seals and sea lions, otters, and whales. In terms of food chains, the mammals are all predators. Certain whales feed on smaller organisms, including molluscs and zooplankton. Otherwise, all eat fish, and their presence and movements in Puget Sound coincide with the seasonal wanderings of large schools of herring and salmon. The fact that marine mammals are generally high in the food chain has made some species vulnerable to toxic contaminants. Puget Sound harbor seals, for example, are known to carry relatively high levels of PCBs in their body fat because they prey on a wide variety of bottom fish that reside in contaminated sediments of Puget Sound's urbanized waterways. Only the fact that other marine mammals, including the orca, prey on fish species that are very mobile during their lives has prevented similar accumulations of toxins in dangerous quantities in their body tissues.

Seals and sea lions

Harbor seals *(Phoca vitulina)* are found throughout the Puget Sound region during all seasons of the year. They are relatively small—males may reach 200 pounds and six feet in length. Harbor seals are mottled gray in color. On land, they frequently resemble logs, perched on rocks with heads and flippers off the surface.

Harbor seals are earless seals, part of a group of seals related to weasels. Their rear flippers serve them well in the water but are useless

on the land. Out of the water, harbor seals move by rocking and rolling. Principal items of the harbor seal diet in Puget Sound are a wide variety of fishes and invertebrates. Harbor seals often are seen near ferry docks, a single head occasionally appearing to stare blankly. Several ferry routes lie close to haulout sites where the animals congregate and breed, including McNeil Island, Protection Island, Race Rocks and Bird Rocks.

The **California sea lion** *(Zalophus californianus)* is the most familiar of the sea lions in appearance. For decades, they have been the performing seal that we have grown accustomed to seeing in circuses and zoos. Before the 1950s, California sea lions were not conspicuous in the Puget Sound marine environment. Remains of California sea lions are known from archaeological sites but the species was unnoticed by early naturalists of Puget Sound. California sea lions that visit Puget Sound all are males, part of a 5,000- to 6,000-member bachelor party of sea lions that migrates to the northeastern Pacific each winter. Puget Sound typically hosts between 1,000 and 2,000 of the animals.

In recent years, these animals have become notorious locally because of their feeding habits. At the Hiram Chittenden Locks, in Seattle, sea lions gather each winter to ambush Lake Washington–bound steelhead. Efforts to control the animals have proven futile. Because the problem is really a population-wide phenomenon and seems to hinge on breeding success in the Channel Islands of Southern California, local efforts will continue to have few results.

Perhaps the ultimate responsibility for the "sea-lion problem" at the locks lies not with the marine mammals, but with the engineers who designed the locks in the 1910s. At that time, there were no steelhead in Lake Washington and apparently no California sea lions in Puget Sound. By creating an artificial shore with no shallow water into which fish could escape from predators, engineers violated a major bioengineering principle now observed in shoreline construction. As in many other cases, the problem is inattention to the ecological consequences of shore modifications, not sea lions eating steelhead.

Other than at the Chittenden Locks, California sea lions can be seen at a variety of Puget Sound locations. They frequent the Edmonds ferry dock in large numbers—ferryboat naturalists have a ringside seat to their favorite haulouts, which are the divers' floats and ferry slip structures just a few yards from the boat.

The **northern,** or **Steller's, sea lion** *(Eumetopias jubatus)* is a visitor to Puget Sound, frequently seen at Edmonds and at other locations on the Sound. Like California sea lions, ours are migrating visitors, here to feed on the Sound's many seasonal delicacies. The northerns arrive in the fall, after leaving the breeding rookeries in Alaska and along the British Columbia coast. Northerns are generally larger than the California sea lions and lighter in color. They are also quieter than their California cousins.

Elephant seals *(Mirounga angustirostris)* are the least common of the pinniped visitors to the Sound. These animals are rarely seen—but easily recognized, because of their unique appearance and awesome bulk. Individuals sighted in the Strait of Juan de Fuca belong to a breeding population at Año Nuevo, on the central California coast.

Otters

Although frequent claims of **sea otters** are made in Puget Sound, there are no wild sea otters in the Sound or in the San Juan Islands. A population of about 75 sea otters does live on the outer Washington coast, where they were introduced in 1969 and 1970. Surprisingly, no records exist for occurrence of the sea otter in the Sound historically. Fur traders acquired the lush skins in abundance from coastal tribes, but frequently remarked on the futility of trading ventures inside the Strait of Juan de Fuca. Sea otters occasionally are sighted near Race Rocks, on the Vancouver Island coast southeast of Victoria, but these animals apparently are wanderers from reintroduced populations farther up the west coast of Vancouver Island. Ferryboat naturalists can see sea otters in captivity at the Pt. Defiance Zoo in Tacoma and the Seattle Aquarium, both within walking distance from ferry terminals.

The **river otter** *(Lutra canadensis)*, on the other hand, is locally abundant in Puget Sound. These sleek mammals like saltwater as much as freshwater and can be seen at certain places playing on floats and docks. Puget Sound shores offer ideal otter habitat, particularly along bluffs. Debris that slumps off steep bluffs sometimes creates cavities around stumps and logs, forming ready-made dens. Otters feed on fish, including sculpin, perch and shellfish.

Whales and dolphins

Cetaceans in Puget Sound provoke the greatest awe of any of our wildlife cohorts. In many respects, they symbolize the Sound at its wildest and most fragile aspects. Both major groups of cetaceans—baleen and toothed whales—are represented here. Some are only incidental visitors; others are permanent residents. Whale sightings represent perhaps the peak experience for the ferryboat naturalist. Circumstances that bring transient animals and transient observers together are uncommon. Nevertheless, your chances of seeing whales are increased directly by the keenness of your observational powers, your perception of appropriate settings and the persistence with which you maintain a likely vantage on the boat. You won't see whales from the coffee shop or when you are snoozing under your newspaper. Think of ferry trips when you don't see whales as training sessions for some inevitable encounter in the future. Eventually, you'll get a show you won't forget.

Baleen whales

Baleen whales represent an adaptation in marine mammals toward the utilization of the ocean's most abundant resources—plankton and small organisms. The baleen whale is toothless. Instead of teeth, its mouth is lined by rows of limber fibrous plates that act as strainers when gulps of water are forced out of the mouth by the tongue.

The most common of the Puget Sound baleen whales is the **Minke whale** *(Balaenoptera acutorostrata)*, a small version of the fin and blue whales that roam the open ocean. Minkes seldom exceed 35 feet in length and appear as streamlined objects arching at the surface of the water in slow, graceful rolls. They are considered common in northern Puget Sound, and frequently seen in tidal convergence zones throughout the San Juans. Minkes feed on shoals of herring and other small fish that concentrate in tide rips and along the eddy lines of current. Their field marks consist of white "arm bands" on their pectoral fins. Their snouts are pointed and the dorsal fins sickle-shaped.

The **California gray whale** *(Eschrichtius robustus)* is a regular visitor to Puget Sound, usually as a solitary animal temporarily sidetracked off the migration route between Baja California, where they give birth during the winter, and the Bering Sea, where they feed during the summer. Individual animals have been reported as appearing to stay through the winter in Puget Sound. These most often are juvenile males. Gray whales are recognized by their mottled, barnacle-covered snouts and by the absence of distinct dorsal fins (they have a series of dorsal bumps). Grays have been reported throughout Puget Sound, but sightings of grays feeding in Puget Sound are uncommon. Their principal places of feeding are in the Bering, Chukchi and Beaufort seas, where they plow deep furrows in the bottom as they dredge for a variety of amphipods and other invertebrates. Feeding gray whales in Puget Sound are limited to a few sites in the Strait of Juan de Fuca.

Humpbacked whales *(Megoptera novaeangliae)* are rare visitors to Puget Sound. Their occasional appearances are unexplained. Humpbacks of the northeast Pacific belong to a population that migrates between southeast Alaska and the Hawaiian Islands. What directs them so far off course is a mystery. Humpbacks have received wide attention because of their acoustic repertoires and dramatic feeding behavior (breeching the water as they rocket upward through a school of forage fish). Although conspicuous in Hawaii and in Alaska, these whales represent some of the most endangered of the Pacific, and virtually nothing is known of their movements between the breeding and feeding grounds.

Toothed whales

At first glance, toothed whales represent a more traditional strategy for food gathering—the familiar pursuit, grasping and chewing common to most mammals. Scientists studying odontocetes (from Greek, "toothed whales") have been startled, however, to find that some species appear to have evolved away from using teeth to grasp or chew. Indeed, in the marine environment, pursuit, grasping and chewing are not easy tasks for large animals preying on small ones, given the fact that whales cannot turn their heads and that prey species are well equipped to outmaneuver the bulky hunters. Evidence is accumulating that supports a different explanation of toothed-whale feeding behavior—one that employs focused beams of intense sound to disorient, stun and even kill their prey.

The **harbor porpoise** *(Phocoena phocoena)* is one of our two species of porpoises: small whales with blunt noses, triangular dorsal fins and spade-shaped teeth. The harbor porpoise is less abundant in Puget Sound than in the past and is considered common only in the northern Sound. Diminutive in scale, the harbor porpoise never exceeds six feet in length. Its coloration is dull gray or brown, without contrasting white patches. This whale is unobtrusive in its behavior, avoiding vessels and other signs of human activity. Ferryboat naturalists will see them only in the distance as they make brief appearances at the surface singly or in small pods. Harbor porpoises feed on schooling fish and squid and prefer to stay in the deeper waterways of the major basins of the Sound when they enter the waters south of Admiralty Inlet.

Dall's porpoise *(Phocoenoides dalli)* is more abundant and far more conspicuous. This little whale seldom exceeds six and one half feet in length. Coloration is black, with a large white patch on the belly and up the flanks of the animal. The trailing edge of the tail-fluke and tip of the dorsal fin also are frequently marked with white. These creatures appear to enjoy approaching a moving vessel. A pod of three to six porpoises often will make its first appearance at some distance from the boat, breaking the surface with a splash. Next, watch the bow wave as they dart to the surface and dive in front of the ship. Because of their black-and-white coloration, Dall's porpoises are mistaken by many as "baby killer whales." When they visit the ship, a crowd gathers at the rail to see the porpoises, which are thrilling in speed and agility. Dall's are often seen on the Port Townsend-Keystone, Port Angeles-Victoria and Seattle-Victoria runs. In addition, they cruise other major channels of the Sound and have been sighted on nearly every ferry route.

Dall's porpoises feed on small schooling fishes and, in the open waters of the North Pacific, gather into great pods—sometimes of several hundred individuals. In Puget Sound, pods seldom exceed a dozen animals, but large groups of as many as 60 have been seen in the Strait of Juan de Fuca.

Dall's porpoises are particularly vulnerable to gill-net fishing. Lethal entanglement kills an estimated 5,000 to 10,000 each year in the North Pacific, primarily in the open-sea drift-net salmon fishery.

The **pilot whale** *(Globicephala macrorhynchus)* is an uncommon visitor to Puget Sound. It is distinguished from the porpoises by its larger size (up to about 22 feet long) and retiring habits. It differs from orcas by the absence of white markings and by its bulbous snout. Pilot whales observed in Puget Sound usually are single animals or in small groups. In the open ocean, however, they frequently travel in large pods. Pilot whales prefer to feed on squid, which helps explain their irregular appearance in Puget Sound.

The **orca whale** *(Orcinus orca)* is the most dramatic of the Puget Sound whales and, to many, a fitting totem-symbol of Puget Sound itself. Traveling in small groups with their distinctive dorsal fins aloft, orcas are a study in power and grace. Mature whales reach 35 feet in length. Males have dorsal fins rising as much as six feet above the back; females have shorter dorsal fins.

Three pods are resident in Puget Sound, the Strait of George and the Strait of Juan de Fuca. These stay relatively close throughout most of the year, feeding primarily on salmon. Several "transient" pods also inhabit Northwest waters, moving along the outer coast and making infrequent visits to the Strait of Juan de Fuca and inland waters. Feeding strategies differ dramatically between the transients and the residents. While residents appear to have developed a distinctive "culture" centered around subsistence on salmon, the transients feed primarily on seals and other marine mammals.

Resident orcas range through Puget Sound and can be seen from any of the ferry routes. But such sightings are not common, even if you spend a lot of time on the water. During the summer and early fall, the orcas concentrate in and around the San Juan Islands, pursuing salmon that move through the archipelago en route to the Nooksack and Fraser rivers. These whales are grouped into three pods: "J" pod, "K" pod and "L" pod.

J pod remains in the inland waters of Puget Sound, the eastern Strait of Juan de Fuca and the Strait of Georgia most of the time. Eighteen orcas currently comprise J pod; the oldest male is Ruffles (J-1), the oldest female is thought to be Granny (J-2). Eleven of the group are females, four are males, and three are juveniles of undetermined sex.

K pod is known to travel to the west coast of Vancouver Island, as well as roam the inner waters. K pod consists of 17 animals, four males, nine females and four orcas of undetermined sex. K pod's oldest males is Sealth (K-5). Tumwater is thought to be Sealth's mother, and the oldest female of the pod.

L pod is the largest of the local resident pods, consisting of 47 individuals. Twelve are known to be males, 22 are females and 13 are of unknown sex. L pod spends most of the time in outer coastal waters off Vancouver Island, making regular visits to the Strait of Juan de Fuca, the San Juans and Puget Sound. Researchers note that L pod displays less tolerance of human activity than the other resident pods, suggesting that they are less habituated to human presence.

The resident pods have been studied for nearly two decades, giving us a remarkably detailed understanding of their natural history. Over the years, researchers have made and catalogued hundreds of photographs of the whales. Distinctive markings on the fins and color-spots are used to identify individuals and give clues to the social organization of the family groups. The picture that emerges is one of remarkable behavior and social fidelity. Family groups center around dominant females—individuals remain with their family groups throughout their lives.

The value of such close-knit kinship groups in terms of feeding strategy is that orcas are able to hunt cooperatively, like lions on the African savannah or wolves of the northern forest and tundra. This highly social behavior is seen in orcas throughout the world. A German researcher once reported a pod of 15 to 20 orcas encircling a pod of about 100 porpoises. After the orcas surrounded the porpoises, one orca would enter the porpoise pod to eat several individuals while the rest of the orcas pod contained the other porpoises. In turn, each orca fed until all the porpoises were consumed.

This type of behavior depends not only on tight social organization, but also on communication. All whales display some degree of vocalization, but in local pods of orcas, vocalization has been elevated to complex sound systems that actually resemble languages, complete with local dialects. Perhaps the most astounding implication of orca vocalization is what some researchers believe is the orca's ability to stun prey with sound—actually issuing a "beam" of sound waves that immobilizes and perhaps kills prey animals outright.

Ironically, the historic abundance of resident orca whales in Puget Sound was a factor in their decline, resulting from exploitation here. As recently as the early 1970s, Puget Sound supplied North America's zoos and marine parks with most of their performing killer whales. Between 1962 and 1976, more than 223 orcas were captured in Washington waters. Ten of these animals died during capture, 31 were retained and about 182 were released. Considering what we now know of orcas' social fidelity, the loss of one third of the population may have long-terms effects on the pods that we will not see for decades. Birth rates among our residents are among the lowest of orcas anywhere in the world. The loss of such a significant genetic resource in the pods may, in fact, doom them.

We celebrate Puget Sound orcas in their stately presence. We marvel at them, the most accessible free orcas on earth. Indeed, we have named them and researchers continued to learn about each of these animals as individuals, who their brothers, mothers and sisters are, whom they play and visit with. Without anthropomorphising, we are seeing them as complex and remarkable organisms, noble and fitting in their marine context. We alone can undo them and we alone can prevent that from happening.

Sightings of a variety of other whales have occurred as scattered incidents throughout Puget Sound. In 1987, **false killer whales** *(Pseudorca crassidens)* were sighted in South Puget Sound. The **Pacific white-sided dolphin** *(Lagenorhynchus obliquidens)* makes regular visits to the Strait of Juan de Fuca and occasionally is seen in the San Juan Islands. This dolphin displays its acrobatic prowess by leaping from the water as it rides the bow wave.

For complete life-history and distribution accounts of these and other marine mammals, see *A Guide to Marine Mammals of Greater Puget Sound.* This guide includes a key to identifying individuals of all three resident orca pods and 28 Minke whales resident in the San Juan Islands.

FERRY ROUTES OF PUGET SOUND

ANDERSON ISLAND

Anderson Island

Puget Sound's southernmost public ferry serves Anderson and Ketron islands just south of the Tacoma Narrows. Operated by Pierce County, the ferry connects the two islands with the town of Steilacoom and gives the ferryboat naturalist a fine glimpse of the South Sound.

The Tacoma Narrows forms a bottleneck both in width and depth of the Sound. At the Narrows Sill, just south of the Narrows Bridge, the bottom rises to about 150 feet in depth. Currents in excess of five knots frequently are encountered on the tide change. This threshold neatly separates the southern basin of Puget Sound from the main basin. Because of the great influx of fresh water from the Nisqually River and many smaller streams, the Narrows Sill also forms a boundary between two sometimes very distinct bodies of water—the saltier, colder water of the main basin and the fresher, warmer water of the southern basin.

This area of the South Sound is important biologically. Shores tend to be less developed and several large areas are managed exclusively as habitat areas. The Nisqually Delta has a large system of salt- and freshwater marshes and is a major stopover for migrating waterfowl and shorebirds. McNeil Island, another critical habitat, is an important harbor seal haulout site. Its "enforced" isolation preserved it as a real refuge from development pressures felt on islands elsewhere throughout Puget Sound.

The 24-minute ride to Anderson Island begins on the Steilacoom waterfront. As you wait to board the ferry, notice the rip-rap shoreline, built to protect the railroad right-of-way from wave erosion. Boulders of pinkish-orange sandstone line this shore for miles. The resulting cobble beach is a poor substitute for the broad sand beach that Steilacoom once boasted.

The complex of piers comprising the ferry dock area form good habitat for pile perch, sculpin and invertebrates such as sunflower stars, mussels and barnacles.

As the ferry pulls away from Steilacoom, you will want to get your bearings. On a clear day, the Tacoma Narrows Bridge is visible to the north, connecting the mainland with the Gig Harbor Peninsula. The shoreline west of the Narrows appears solid but is actually broken by Hale Passage, which separates Fox Island from the Gig Harbor Peninsula. Gibson Point, at the southern tip of Fox Island, is marked by a beacon flashing at four-second intervals. Carr Inlet separates Fox Island from McNeil Island with its conspicuous yellow prison complex.

Anderson Island, the ferry's destination, lies across Balch Passage from McNeil Island. Eagle Island, a 10-acre state park, sits several hundred yards off Anderson Island in Balch Passage.

The nearest point of land on Anderson Island is Yoman Point.

Within a few minutes of leaving Steilacoom, notice the extensive gravel-mining operation along the eastern shore north of the ferry and just north of the mouth of Chambers Creek. Commercial operators have quarried gravel here for nearly 80 years, digging into deposits of a broad formation of gravel known as the Steilacoom Delta.

Using binoculars, you can see bedding patterns on some of the exposed quarry faces. Downward tilting beds suggest that the gravel was deposited underwater on the sloping face of a river delta. Although an exact picture of the events that formed the Steilacoom Delta is difficult to paint, the delta formed along the shore of a vast lake whose water level was rising. The source of the gravel comprising the delta was apparently an early Puyallup River, considerably larger than the present one because it contained runoff from several large Cascade foothills watersheds.

Directly south of the ferry route is Ketron Island, which has its own ferry service described later. About eight minutes out of Steila-

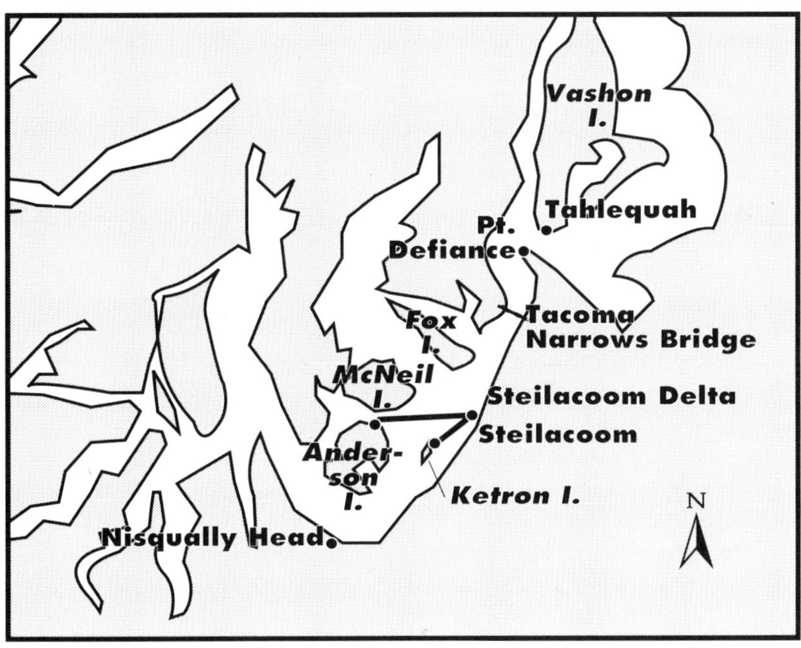

coom, the ferry clears the northern tip of Ketron, and the view toward the Nisqually Delta opens. The Nisqually River is the fifth-largest river entering Puget Sound and the largest to enter the southern basin. The channel across the front of the delta is the Nisqually Reach. Ships moving to the docks of Olympia and Shelton must pass through the narrow channel between the southern shore of Anderson Island and the Nisqually Delta. Unless dredged, Nisqually Reach eventually will be closed off by advancing river deposits. The process probably will require many centuries, but as long as the Nisqually Glacier continues to grind the flanks of Mt. Rainier and the silt-laden runoff pours down the Nisqually River, it is inevitable.

As the ferry moves closer to Anderson Island, the looming presence of Mt. Rainier south of Steilacoom becomes more apparent. What we see of Mt. Rainier includes the Tahoma, North Mowich, South Mowich, Edmunds and Puyallup glaciers and three visible summits—Liberty Cap (on the north), Columbia Crest (in the center—the highest) and Point Success (on the south). From the ferry, this point—the 14,410-foot summit of Columbia Crest—is about 43 miles away, as an adventurous crow would fly.

Past Ketron Island, the ferry passes over the deepest "hole" in southern Puget Sound. Water depth here approaches 600 feet. Tide rips are sometimes apparent as tidal currents of the Narrows encounter the movement of deeper water in the basin. Current measurements taken just off Anderson Island reveal surface flow primarily to the north; bottom currents flow to the southeast. The only hint we have from the deck of the boat is the texture of the water surface and the eddies and whirlpools of converging currents.

Look out for Dall's porpoises; ferry crews report occasional sightings throughout the year. The diminutive black-and-white cetaceans play in the ferry's wake. Other marine mammals include harbor seals (the McNeil Island herd) and California sea lions. Northern sea lions and Minke whales are rarities.

Birds on the Anderson Island run include rhinoceros auklets during the spring and summer. Hordes of gulls may be seen attacking herring balls. Generally speaking, diving birds are found closer to the shores. Near Anderson Island look for bald eagles perching in trees. A migrant brown pelican was observed near the Anderson Island ferry dock, where it lingered for several weeks one autumn.

As the boat nears Anderson Island, notice the gentle beach near the ferry dock. Longshore currents converge here, bringing sediment both from eroding shores at Yoman Point and from along Balch Passage.

Ketron Island

The ride to Ketron Island lasts only about 12 minutes, but it takes us along the shore south of Steilacoom into Cormorant Passage where we share, for a moment, the private world of this small island and its discrete setting.

Ketron was named Long Island in the journal of George Vancouver. Vancouver and his longboat crew slept here the night of May 26, 1792 as they returned to the *Discovery* from a charting excursion of Nisqually Reach. Vancouver's name is appropriate—this mile-and-a-half-long island consists of a long ridge that runs parallel to the eastern shore. If you took the water out of the Sound, Ketron would appear to be a little ridge perched along a deep valley separating it from Anderson Island. The "valley" is the southern end of a deep basin situated between Nisqually Reach and the Tacoma Narrows.

As the ferry pulls away from the Steilacoom dock it runs along the shore toward Gordon Point, with its unusual marina (a "bottomless" building on piers—boats are hoisted into the rafters). The city of Steilacoom maintains a small park on the beach north of Gordon Point. Past Gordon Point, the ferry heads into Cormorant Passage. This quiet pass is relatively undeveloped owing to upland ownership by the U.S. Army. Like the Steilacoom waterfront, the shore is lined with rip-rap to protect the railroad.

The northern tip of Ketron supports an extensive kelp bed during summer and fall. Bull kelp requires a cobble or rock bottom and forms thick forests underwater, which provide shelter and food for many fish and invertebrates. Wildlife here is similar to that on the Anderson Island run, including eagles, diving seabirds and perhaps kingfishers and herons.

PT. DEFIANCE

The brief ferry ride between Tahlequah, on the south end of Vashon Island, and Pt. Defiance reveals some historic glimpses of the Puget Sound shore. The dark forests of Pt. Defiance Park present a torn skyline of ancient broken snags and weather-flagged trees. Such descriptions were a conspicuous part of every explorer's account of the inland sea. From here Vancouver had a dramatic glimpse of Mt. Rainier. He wrote: "...we found the inlet to terminate here in an extensive circular compact bay [modern Commencement Bay], whose waters washed the base of mount [*sic*] Rainier."

The historic flavor of Pt. Defiance still can be sampled in Pt. Defiance Park. Here, the city of Tacoma preserved almost 700 acres of timber and shoreline in its natural state. Nearly two miles of public-access beach line the dark prominence. You can visit Fort Nisqually, a replica of the Hudson Bay Company outpost that served as administrative hub of early-day Puget Sound. For the ferryboat naturalist

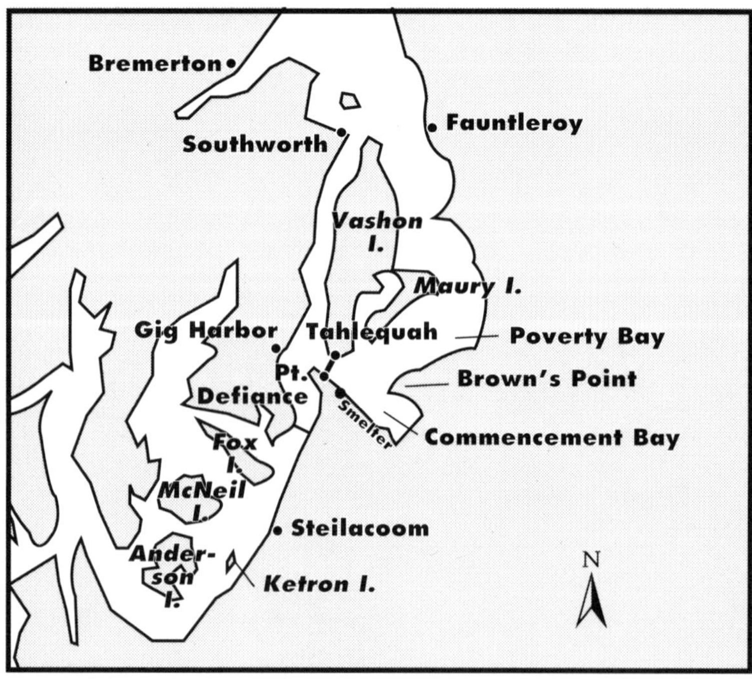

ashore, the Pt. Defiance Aquarium offers outstanding opportunities to view Puget Sound fishes and invertebrates.

The Pt. Defiance-to-Tahlequah ferry crosses Dalco Passage, which runs east and west, separating Vashon Island from the mainland. A short distance to the west it bends around the sharp elbow of Point Defiance. The Brothers and Mt. Constance are prominent peaks of the Olympic Mountains that rise above Gig Harbor Peninsula along the western horizon. Colvos Passage—the western channel separating Vashon Island from the mainland—enters from the north to the west of Vashon. To the east lie Quartermaster Harbor and East Passage, the main channel of the Sound.

As the ferry pulls away from the Pt. Defiance dock, notice an unusual rock formation, the point of land enclosing the marina to the east. The material is a remnant of the smelter waste generated over decades at the Tacoma Smelter at Ruston. Although the man-made landform is solid, wave erosion gnaws into it at the waterline.

As the ferry clears the point, the view east into Commencement Bay unfolds. On clear days, the regal form of Mt. Rainier dominates, reminding us of Vancouver's impression of its closeness. Although we know Rainier is about 45 miles away, its connection to Puget Sound is very real. Meltwater from each of the major glaciers you see from this vantage flows into the Sound, and each watershed contributes runoff, silt, and waste to the marine waterway.

Commencement Bay received its name in 1841 from Lt. Charles Wilkes, whose expedition "commenced" its south Puget Sound survey from a point in the harbor. At that time, Commencement Bay was lined by vast wetlands at the Puyallup River's mouth. Today, in contrast, the mouth of the Puyallup forms one of Puget Sound's busiest seaports. The great system of marshes, sloughs and tideflats, which by one estimate covered more than 2,400 acres, now amounts to only 125 acres.

Although not visible from such a distance, the Commencement Bay harbor system consists of seven channels maintained for port facilities. In their midst is the mouth of the Puyallup River, which flows from the snout of the Puyallup Glacier on Mt. Rainier. Hylebos Creek, another of the waterways, originates near Milton and has an important remnant of wetland habitat in its upper reaches.

Commencement Bay earned a dubious distinction as one of Puget Sound's most polluted areas. The waterway endured decades of abuse, including dumping of sewage, industrial waste and contaminated dredge spoils.

North of Commencement Bay, notice a prominent, gently rounded hill: Brown's Point. The name is used locally to refer to the entire hill district as well as the tip of land along the shore. The exact location of

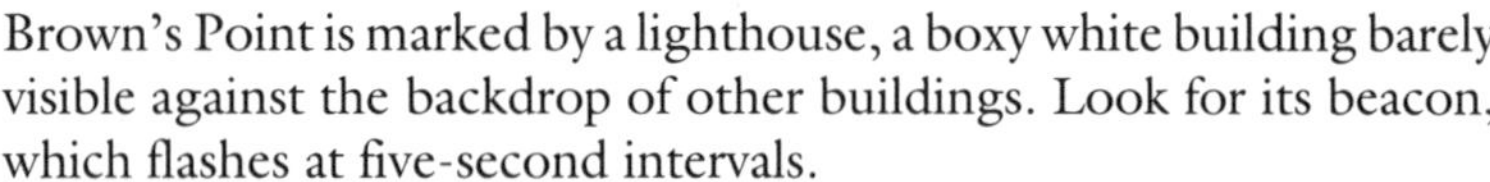

Brown's Point is marked by a lighthouse, a boxy white building barely visible against the backdrop of other buildings. Look for its beacon, which flashes at five-second intervals.

East Passage, the main channel of Puget Sound, enters from the north between Brown's Point and Maury Island. In the distance you see Dash Point and the curving shore of Poverty Bay. Pt. Robinson forms the eastern tip of Maury Island, Vashon's smaller partner.

Maury Island and Vashon Island are separated by an inlet called Quartermaster Harbor, named by Wilkes in an uncharacteristic fit of whimsy as a "haven for petty officers' spirits." Today, the picturesque inlet serves boat owners' and shore residents' spirits as a fine moorage and quiet residential setting.

West of the ferry, the Sound appears to dead-end against the solid, forested wall of the Gig Harbor Peninsula shore. The narrow entrance to Gig Harbor is visible just north of Pt. Defiance. Puget Sound continues south around the corner of Pt. Defiance, reaching its narrowest point—The Tacoma Narrows. Colvos Passage enters just beyond Pt. Dalco, the southwestern tip of Vashon Island. Rather than a "dead end," this area is an important junction in the Sound—where violent currents mix, creating a rich biological environment. As the tide ebbs here, a large eddy forms north of Pt. Defiance, pushed by the incredible surge of water through the Tacoma Narrows. These waters collide with currents in Dalco Passage, which run to the west on both the flood and ebb tides.

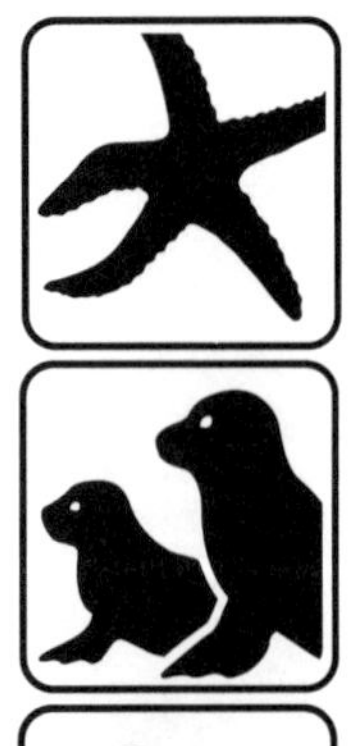

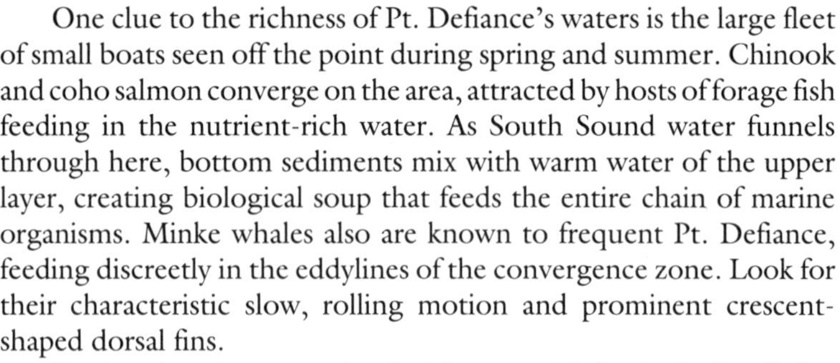

One clue to the richness of Pt. Defiance's waters is the large fleet of small boats seen off the point during spring and summer. Chinook and coho salmon converge on the area, attracted by hosts of forage fish feeding in the nutrient-rich water. As South Sound water funnels through here, bottom sediments mix with warm water of the upper layer, creating biological soup that feeds the entire chain of marine organisms. Minke whales also are known to frequent Pt. Defiance, feeding discreetly in the eddylines of the convergence zone. Look for their characteristic slow, rolling motion and prominent crescent-shaped dorsal fins.

During the winter months, the Narrows vicinity, including Dalco Passage, hosts large flocks of gulls and diving birds, such as common murres, ancient murrelets, Bonaparte's gulls, mew gulls and other seabirds.

As the boat approaches the Vashon shore, notice the lush stands of sun-loving madrona that line the south-facing bluffs of the island. Madrona thrives on dry, gravelly soil and requires full sunlight. Bluffs that rim Puget Sound offer ideal habitat for this relative of rhododendron. Bulkheads guard the beach houses crowded along the shore.

Strong currents move along the Tahlequah shoreline, carrying sediments from east to west. The gently-indented cove has a sandy bottom; eelgrass beds line the nearshore area. Watch for river otters, which are common in the area.

The single-lane Tahlequah dock is distinctively quaint among Puget Sound ferry terminals. Look for cormorants on the weathered pilings of the one-lane pier, draping their wings to dry. Ubiquitous rock doves (pigeons) and crows reside here and forage along the walkway.

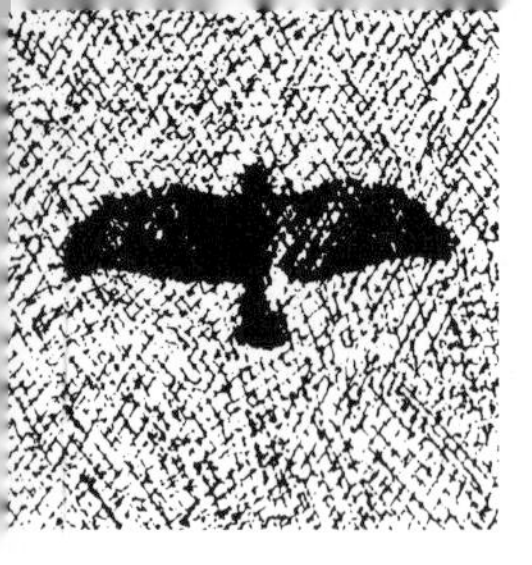

FAUNTLEROY/ VASHON/ SOUTHWORTH

South of Seattle, Vashon Island splits Puget Sound into two major channels—East Passage (east of the island) and Colvos Passage (west of the island). Ferries of the Fauntleroy-Vashon-Southworth route connect the northern tip of Vashon Island with Fauntleroy Cove on the eastern shore and Point Southworth on the western shore. On this route, the ferryboat naturalist crosses the main basin of the Sound, midway along its longest fetch. With prevailing winds from the south, seas are well formed by the time they pass Vashon's northern tip. And they still have more than 30 miles in which to build before colliding with Whidbey Island to the north.

Fauntleroy Cove

Fauntleroy Cove is a small dimple between Brace Point to the south and the steep forested bluff of Point Williams just to the north. Lincoln Park, with its cobble shoreline and towering forest, lines the Point Williams shore. South of the ferry dock, houses of the aging Seattle neighborhood line the shore with a curious mix of bulkheads. The ferry dock extends quite a distance over the water—Fauntleroy Cove is not particularly deep.

The view from Fauntleroy takes in the northern reach of East Passage, the southernmost extended fetch of the main basin. The waves generated here in a good southwesterly blow will be felt to Alki Point and beyond, all the way to Whidbey Island. Vashon Island sits in the middle distance, with Dolphin Point the nearest point of land. South along the Vashon shore, Maury Island protrudes like a broad wing, tipped by Robinson Point. On the eastern shore, Three Tree Point juts out conspicuously 4.5 nautical miles to the south.

The ferry dock on Vashon is visible just east of Point Vashon, the island's northern tip. Point Southworth is visible in the gap between Point Vashon and Blake Island, the dark and inviting isle toward the northwest. Beyond Blake, in the distance, is the entrance to Rich Passage and the south shore of Bainbridge Island. Restoration Point, named by Captain George Vancouver in honor of the restoration of the English monarchy following the Cromwell era, is the southwestern tip of Bainbridge Island. A beacon there marks Decatur Reef, where, during winter 1855-1856, the U.S. sloop-of-war *Decatur* was grounded.

FAUNTLEROY/VASHON/SOUTHWORTH

As the ferry clears Fauntleroy Dock look for ducks and seabirds resting in the calm of Fauntleroy Cove. Once the boat is out of the shallow inlet, Alki Point lighthouse, with its five-second flash, is clearly visible to the north. In heavy weather look for a longshore sediment plume along the eastern shore. Net flow of sediments is to the north and wave energy is high along the northwest-trending shore north of Fauntleroy toward Alki Point. The ride to Vashon lasts about 15 minutes.

Approaching Vashon, look for seabirds off the island's north shore. Allen Bank extends as a shelf about 70 feet deep for nearly a mile north of Point Vashon. The bank is known to salmon fishermen for its hefty chinooks, fished particularly during winter and early spring.

The name Vashon was applied by Vancouver in honor of James Vashon, a Royal Navy captain he served in the West Indies prior to the voyage of *Discovery*. We see the name used frequently to describe the most widespread geological formation in the Puget Sound region—the Vashon sediments of the Fraser Glaciation.

The Fraser Glaciation was the last of as many as six glacial inundations of the Puget Sound region. It corresponds directly with the Wisconsin Glaciation of the upper Midwest—roughly 15,000 years before the present. Named for the Fraser River of British Columbia, this event occurred when many large glaciers in mountain

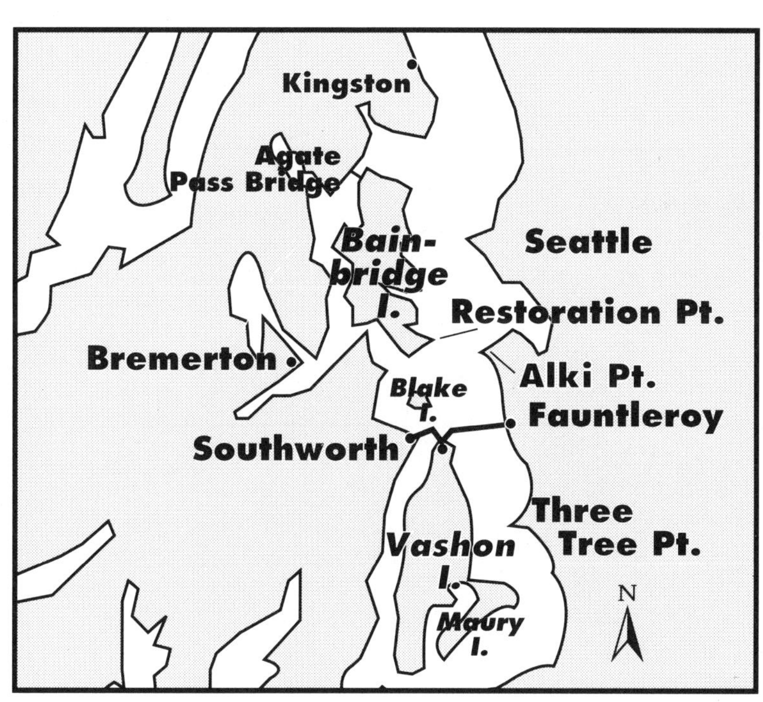

valleys of the British Columbia Coast Range fused into one vast ice tongue that swept over Vancouver Island and into the structural trough between the Cascade and Olympic ranges.

Within the Fraser Glaciation period, the ice front advanced and retreated several times. Each advance is called a "stade." The Vashon Stade was the most extensive onslaught of ice into the Puget Sound area. As the ice front advanced, meltwater streams poured out of its broad snout and flowed across the gravel-strewn lowland, carrying large quantities of sand, pebbles and cobbles. As the glacier grew southward, it covered its earlier outwash with fresh deposits of unsorted gravel and debris and compressed all of the material beneath its mighty bulk. With the retreat of the glacier, more outwash debris piled atop the compressed layer. Taken together, the outwash sands, till and other material created a gravel blanket as much as 150 feet thick, which covers the entire Puget Lowland. The material is visible in profile where the invading sea has eroded into the soft deposits.

Throughout the Puget Sound region, the name Vashon provokes different reactions from those who must deal with its glacial legacy. To the backyard gardener with a tender back, the compressed gravel and clay of the Vashon till is disdainfully cursed as "hardpan." To the

planner and civil engineer, landslides and slope erosion that inevitably follow improper siting on slopes of Vashon debris are a reminder of the costs of building on the stuff. Had he known that the name would be applied to Puget Sound's principal species of gravel, Vancouver might have thought to memorialize his former commander differently.

Departing Vashon, the ferry heads across the northern end of Colvos Passage, named in 1841 by Lt. Wilkes for Midshipman George W. Colvocoressis. Colvos Passage is about 14 miles in length and has its southern end at Dalco Passage, opposite and north of Pt. Defiance. Look for kelp beds off the beach near Pt. Vashon. Moving from the lee of Vashon Island, any southerly breeze is immediately noticed as it funnels up the narrow pass. Robust current rips are also common here as water passes around and over Allen Bank and currents running on both sides of Vashon Island collide.

Crossing Colvos Passage requires only about eight minutes, barely enough time to fully appreciate the view of Blake Island, all of its 475 acres a state park. Access is by boat—either private craft or scheduled tour boat from the Seattle waterfront.

As the ferry approaches Pt. Southworth, look for pigeon guillemots near the shore. A nesting population inhabits the soft bluff along the point during late spring and summer months. Loons, scoters and grebes also are present.

Notice two distinct shades of rock in the bluff face south of the ferry dock. Two types of sediments are visible in Pt. Southworth, and both predate Vashon glacial debris by as much as 100,000 years. The lower layer, about 20 feet thick, is called the Double Bluff formation. Double Bluff sediments are named for a headland on Whidbey Island and thought to be 200,000 to 300,000 years of age. The upper 40 feet consist of Whidbey formation debris, about 100,000 to 150,000 years old. Double Bluff materials, found in several places along the shores of Puget Sound, apparently were deposits on the bottom of a great glacial lake. Whidbey formation sediments were apparently deposited on a broad floodplain during a warmer period of history. Elsewhere in Puget Sound, layers of peat are associated with Whidbey sediments.

The shore at Southworth is a generous beach with extensive sand bottom beneath the ferry dock. This is the deposition area for a longshore transport regime that carries sediment north along the western shore of Colvos Passage and deposits it in the quieter water just north of Pt. Southworth. Pile perch are visible in and around the pilings. Look carefully at the bottom here for soles and flounders, Dungeness crabs and skates. Against the light sand bottom, fish are fairly conspicuous. Just offshore, eelgrass beds line the gently sloping bottom.

SEATTLE/ BREMERTON

The Seattle-Bremerton ferry run is Puget Sound's lunch-bucket ferry ride, conveying commuters both directions—to jobs in Seattle from homes in quieter Kitsap County and from homes in Seattle to the Puget Sound Naval Shipyard in Bremerton. Despite the atmosphere of routine inside the cabin, outside—along the deck rail—Seattle-to-Bremerton is a naturalist's delight. We see the full sweep of Elliott Bay and Alki Point, cross the main fetch of the central Sound and enter the narrow surging channel of Rich Passage as, expectantly, we seek the inner recesses of Sinclair Inlet and the familiar gray cranes and gantries of Bremerton's boilerplated waterfront. Only the San Juan Islands require a more attentive watch, if we are to take in everything that such a varied land- and seascape offers.

This 50-minute crossing begins at Puget Sound's historic crossroads of water traffic, Colman Dock. Today's spare architecture, trim dockworks and gleaming superferries do little to convey the legacy of a place that once mothered a brood of smoke-belching packet steamers known as the Mosquito Fleet. With comings and goings to rival a major midwestern railroad station, passenger and freight ships with names like the *Indianapolis* and the *Whatcom* hovered at dockside, dropped lines and glided quickly to thriving Puget Sound ports like Fairhaven, Dockton and Utsalady. Today's choices are simpler—Winslow or Bremerton—and the rides, for those not intent on being naturalists, are a lot like riding a very wide city bus.

As the boat glides from its slip, look to the south of the ferry terminal. Before there was a Seattle, a prominent little point of land protruded from the shore several blocks south of what became Colman Dock. Behind the graceful hook of Piner's Point was a shallow cove, lush with eelgrass beds. Because most of Seattle was either too steep for building, or awash at high tide, the city brought in fill to swallow the cove and the eelgrass.

South of Piner's Point, miles of mudflats lined the broad mouth of the Duwamish River. Originally the river flowed onto the mudflats about $1^1/_2$ miles south of the present shoreline of Harbor Island. At the time of the Wilkes exploration, in 1841, four islands formed the Duwamish Delta. The Duwamish was the collective name for several tributary streams: the Cedar, the Green and the Black rivers, which drained the Cedar River valley, the Kent Valley and Lake Washington, respectively. In 1916, the Montlake Cut and the Lake Washington ship canal were opened. The result was that Lake Washington was lowered by eight feet, and the Cedar River (previously flowing to the Duwamish) turned into the old lake outlet channel of the Black River and flowed into Lake Washington. No longer the outlet of Lake Washington, the Black River dried up. Harbor Island, visible today with its ranks of container-ship cranes, was created from fill (Vashon Glaciation sediments) sluiced down from nearby Beacon Hill.

Look for gulls near the waterfront. The bustle of crowds and the lure of easy pickings from garbage cans and big-hearted outdoor diners keep the gull population along the Elliott Bay waterfront very stable. Western grebes frequently work the nearshore areas, benefitting from the exposure of schools of forage fish in deeper water.

The ferry eases toward Duwamish Head, the promontory that marks the northeastern tip of the West Seattle peninsula. To the north, across the open mouth of Elliott Bay, Magnolia Bluff and West Point line the northern shore of Seattle's harbor. Dead ahead, on the distant shore of Bainbridge Island, is the entrance to Port Blakely, another of Puget Sound's colorful historical places. In its heyday, Blakely bustled with lumber-laden windjammers and its own shipyard turned out some of the most beautiful tall ships to grace the North Pacific. Guarding the entrance to Port Blakely is a pile of rocks called Blakely Rock.

As the ferry passes Duwamish Head, notice the angle of attack of the waves. With the prevailing southwesterly weather patterns, waves in the inner harbor of Elliott Bay will come from the west. South winds in the main channel of the sound create waves that move almost due

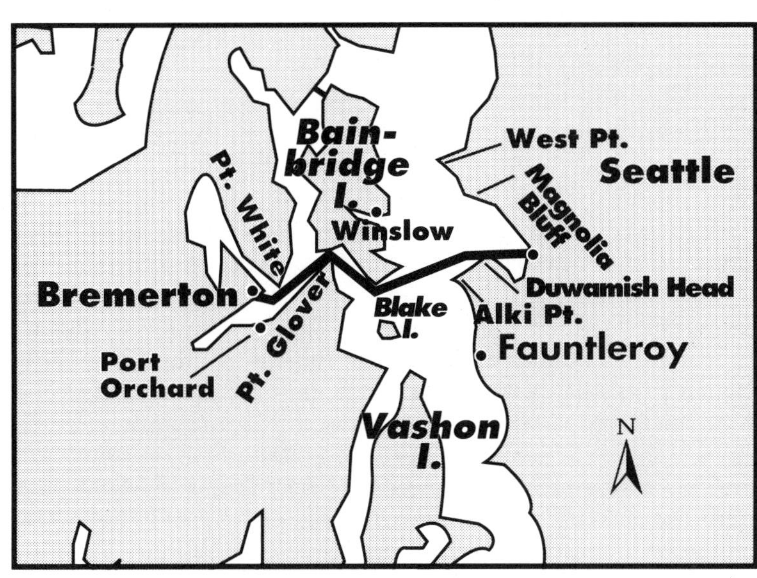

north until they bend around Alki Point in a process called wave refraction. Deep within Elliott Bay, waves will have bent nearly 90 degrees. Notice the change in wave angle as the boat nears Alki Beach and finally clears Alki Point.

Just off Duwamish Head, Alki Point comes into view along the broad curving shore of Alki Beach. The word "Alki" comes from the Chinook Jargon and has various meanings: "by and by" or "soon." Settlers who landed here in 1851 applied the name as a vote of confidence for the future of their settlement. The name was later adopted as the Washington State motto.

By and by, the ferry passes north of a horn buoy and changes course to the south. This slight turn occurs about seven minutes out of Colman Dock. Notice that the bow is now headed just off the southeastern point of land on Bainbridge Island: Restoration Point. Capt. George Vancouver named this point in honor of the restoration of the English monarchy that followed Oliver Cromwell's death. Vancouver anchored off the point between May 19 and May 30, 1792.

About 12 minutes out of Seattle, the ferry slips between Alki Point on the south and West Point on the north and begins crossing the main channel. The boat will settle into a slight roll for this crossing as it moves parallel to waves generated by prevailing winds from the south.

To the south, the Sound splits into two channels around Vashon Island. The eastern channel is East Passage; the western channel is Colvos Passage. Blake Island occupies the foreground.

To the north, the long fetch of the Sound's central basin recedes in the distance. The south shore of Whidbey Island is visible about 24 miles away. Port Blakely and Blakely Rock are in the foreground. North of Blakely Rock, look for Wing Point, which encloses the entrance to Eagle Harbor. The town of Winslow, another ferry destination, is tucked away on the hillside north of the harbor.

About 20 minutes out of Seattle, the ferry passes Restoration Point, with its parklike south shore and low ochre bluffs. Vancouver's journal mentions that Indians gathered on the luxuriant meadows for the purpose of gathering roots—probably camas or wild onions. What appears to be a meadow now is, in fact, a golf course. Kelp beds line the end of the point; eelgrass grows along the beach to the west. Notice the currents becoming apparent here. During Vancouver's visit to Restoration Point, a swiftly-flowing ebb tide issuing from Rich Passage forced the *Discovery* to move to more secure anchorage. The westbound ferry passes almost exactly over that anchorage once it is opposite the bluff west of the open space on Restoration Point.

The ferry is headed toward a prominent point of land to the southwest. This is Orchard Point, marked by a horn and a light. The ferry slows as it approaches the entrance to Rich Passage. The conspicuous terrace of rocks at Orchard Point and at Restoration Point is of the same general formation of Blakely Rock, seen earlier. These rocks are all part of an older marine terrace, once eroded by waves, now uplifted slightly.

The ferry turns along the south side of Bainbridge Reef, marked with a light and bellbuoy. Entering Rich Passage, you pass Clam Bay, on the south shore just inside Orchard Point and the low forms of Orchard Rocks along the north side of the channel. The point of land opposite Orchard Rocks is called Middle Point. Several salmon pens can be seen floating in the waterway. Look for large flocks of black-headed Bonaparte gulls during spring months, along with rafts of scoters and loons. Keep an eye out for eagles in the treetops as the boat passes through the narrow channel. Strong eddies occur between Middle Point and Pt. Glover, ahead on the south.

About 36 minutes from Seattle, Rich Passage takes a sharp turn south as it rounds Pt. Glover. Point White constricts the passage on the west side. Between Pt. Glover and Pt. White, massive eddies form on the tide change, further constricting the stream. Navigators report rare currents of 6 knots here. Given its strong currents and narrow width, this area can be very interesting—with the added excitement of passing an aircraft carrier from the Bremerton naval shipyard!

Within a few minutes of passing Pt. Glover on the south, the ferry cruises past Waterman Point. The large waterway opening to the northwest is the northern branch of Port Orchard, which separates Bainbridge Island from the mainland on the west.

Ahead is the southern branch of Port Orchard, with the Bremerton shipyard visible on one side and scattered houses visible along the other shore. About 45 minutes from Seattle, the boat passes Point Herron, visible to the west. The tapering arm of Sinclair Inlet lies ahead to the southwest. Passing Pt. Herron, you can see the narrow channel of the Port Washington Narrows, which connects to Dyes Inlet, an extensive waterway to the northwest. The Manette Bridge over Port Washington Narrows connects the community of East Bremerton with the city of Bremerton.

About 50 minutes into the ferry ride, the boat makes its last turn toward the ferry dock alongside the Puget Sound Naval Shipyard. Surprisingly, both glaucous-winged gulls and pigeon guillamots nest along this intensively built shore.

SEATTLE/ WINSLOW

The Seattle-to-Winslow run is one of the most heavily traveled routes of Puget Sound. Each day, thousands of somnolent commuters file on and off the boats that cross the waters of Elliott Bay and connect suburban Winslow, on Bainbridge Island, with downtown Seattle. During the 30-minute crossing you get a good look at the Seattle skyline contrasted against the backdrop of the Cascades, the Olympics rising over the forested slopes of Bainbridge Island, and views up and down the long open fetch of the central Sound. Distant ferryboats are visible on the Bremerton and Fauntleroy runs; overhead, jet aircraft make their final approach turns to Sea-Tac Airport (10 miles to the south) and ships move to and from their berths on the busy waterfront. Yet for all of the commotion of the surroundings, and the detachment of the commuters, the ferry glides across a marine wilderness, where creatures as varied as jellyfish and orca whales make their home, and natural forces prevail.

Elliott Bay

Elliott Bay is Puget Sound's busiest seaport, center of the Puget Sound marine transportation network. The decades have seen shifts in the types of freight moved over waterfront docks, and their destinations, but Elliott Bay has consistently been the commercial gateway between Seattle and the world beyond. It saw the era of lumber schooners, when the forests fell and sawmills hummed along the waterfront. It endured the Alaska gold rush and gave Seattle its reputation as "Alaska's largest city." It was home port to the Mosquito Fleet, the armada of trim steamers that connected the Sound's far reaches with commercial Seattle. Its importance to the economy of the Pacific Northwest dictated that it would be shaped to meet the needs of commerce.

As a result, the shoreline of Elliott Bay has been transformed. Even the topography of the uplands surrounding it is altered. Skyscrapers tower where brooding fir trees once stood. Some of Seattle's hills were leveled to accommodate the burgeoning city. But if the urban shoreline appears devoid of natural character, nature doesn't give up easily—the downtown Seattle waterfront sports a nesting colony of about 100 pairs of glaucous-winged gulls and teems with marine wildlife.

To the northwest is Magnolia Bluff, so named in 1856 by Capt. George Davidson of the U.S. Coast Survey because he thought he was seeing magnolia trees. In fact, he was seeing madronas, the sun-loving broad-leaf evergreens that are common throughout the Sound region. The lowland separating Magnolia from the city is called Interbay. Originally, a wedge-shaped cove known as Smith Cove formed the outlet to wetlands of the Interbay area. Today, Smith Cove is covered with fill and is heavily industrialized.

East of the Interbay area is Queen Anne Hill. Between Queen Anne and what is now the heart of downtown Seattle the skyline once rose along another hilltop. Leveled in the early 1900s, this area is now called the Denny Regrade. The gently curving shoreline of the Seattle waterfront is entirely seawalled and wharf-covered. For gulls, grebes and other fish-eating birds, the seawall means that water is deep right up to the shore and fish cannot escape into the shallower water to avoid predators. Gulls also are attracted to food provided by people—be it french fries or errant organic jetsam.

South of the ferry terminal (Colman Dock), the view is dominated by the Kingdome and—when the weather cooperates—Mt. Rainier (14,410 ft.). The blue shadows of 4,000-ft. Willis Wall on Rainier's north face give the mountain a dramatic aspect from this perspective. Poking over Rainier's eastern shoulder is Little Tahoma, small in comparison to the summit of Rainier itself, but, at 11,117 ft., Washington's third-highest summit.

Harbor Island flanks the southern shore of Elliott Bay. It is one of the largest man-made islands in the world, covering about 1,400 acres. The fill to create the island was dredged from the tide flats that extended for more than a mile between the original mouth of the Duwamish River and the modern harbor. The two channels, East and

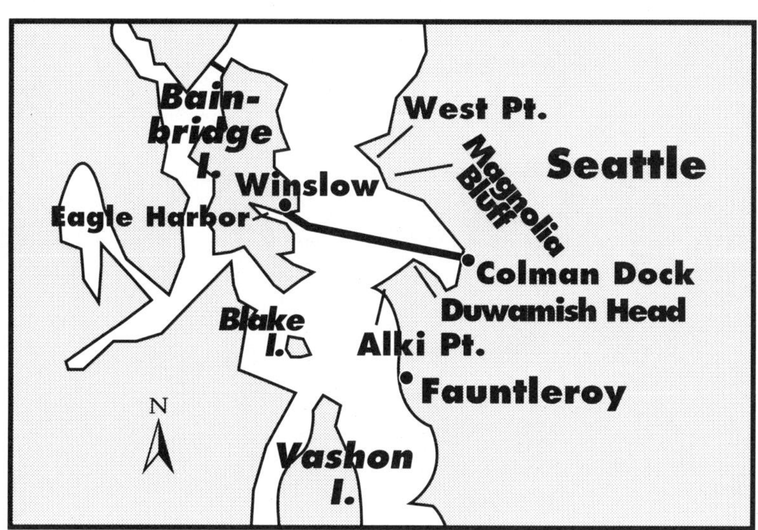

West waterways, allow ships access to the docks. Large orange cranes mark the Port of Seattle's container-ship terminals. The graceful arc of the West Seattle Bridge looms as a backdrop.

The high land mass west of Harbor Island is West Seattle. Ferries once plied the water between West Seattle and downtown. In fact, Puget Sound's first ferry boat, the *City of Seattle,* inaugurated ferry service on the Sound with its West Seattle run beginning in 1888. Owned by the West Seattle Land and Improvement Company, the boat made as many as 10 runs daily (fare: five cents) and spurred a land boom in West Seattle (the owners ran the ferry at a loss as long as property sold briskly). Eventually, ferry service was discontinued because of competition from streetcars, which began service in 1907, crossing the Duwamish mudflats on a long trestle. Duwamish Head, the prominent headland on the northeastern tip of West Seattle, was the ferry destination. The ferry terminal on the Seattle side was at the present-day foot of Marion Street, one block north of Colman Dock.

Beyond Duwamish Head, the long, gentle crescent of Alki Beach arcs to the southwest. This beach undergoes dramatic changes in its profile and composition through the cycle of seasons. During summer, it traps large quantities of sand, becoming a broad strand just right for recreation. In the winter, however, intensified wave energy scours the beach, revealing a steep, narrow beach of cobbles.

Central Basin of the Sound

As the ferry crosses between Alki Point and West Point, it enters the central basin of the Sound. In this busy thoroughfare, ships move to and from the ports of Tacoma, Olympia and Shelton. This is also the principal fetch within the Sound—the area where waves are formed by winds. As typical low-pressure weather systems move in from the Pacific, winds enter the Puget Trough around the southern Olympics from the southwest. During high-pressure systems—cold and clear in winter; clear and balmy in summer—winds reverse and come from the north. Because of the north-south axis of the Sound, winds from either direction are funneled along the water to create waves. These waves are able to build and carry their momentum for long distances because of the mechanics of wave energy. Where they collide directly with soft bluffs of glacial debris, their erosive power is particularly strong. Where they collide at an angle, these waves drive sediments along the shore, resulting in the low spit formations typified by West Point and Alki Point. During typical northerly or southerly "blows," the ferry will cross the path of the waves, resulting in a slight but noticeable rocking of the boat.

Blakely Rock

Visible in the distance against the dark outline of Bainbridge Island is Blakely Rock. This rockpile is composed of the same type of rocks found on Restoration Point (the southeastern tip of Bainbridge Island) and several other points of land in the vicinity. These are all remnants of a raised marine terrace. Marine terraces are, typically, old surfaces shaped by wave action when sea level was higher than at the present. Immediately west of Blakely Rock is the entrance to Blakely Harbor.

Port Blakely, a once-thriving town located on Blakely Harbor, was one of Puget Sound's most important early mill sites. When towering firs still reached water's edge, saws humming at Port Blakely created shipload after shipload

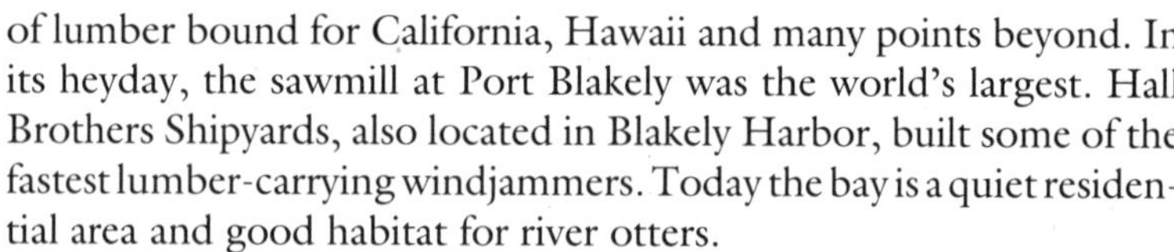

of lumber bound for California, Hawaii and many points beyond. In its heyday, the sawmill at Port Blakely was the world's largest. Hall Brothers Shipyards, also located in Blakely Harbor, built some of the fastest lumber-carrying windjammers. Today the bay is a quiet residential area and good habitat for river otters.

About 20 minutes out of Seattle, the ferry makes a hard turn north, around a buoy. This marks the approach to Eagle Harbor and Winslow, the ferry's destination. The ferry takes a seemingly indirect route approaching Eagle Harbor because of an extensive shoal southeast of Wing Point and because of a reef that juts southward from its tip. By staying well to the south and rounding the buoy, the ferry follows a channel of deeper water.

The bluff just west of the ferry rises above Rockaway Beach. Much of the shore along Rockaway is modified by the construction of seawalls that protect upland residential property. The predominant longshore current here runs north. Kelp beds line the nearshore, indicating a cobble bottom.

At about 25 minutes, the ferry enters Eagle Harbor. Wing Point, to the east, is festooned with an assortment of pricey homes and an odd collection of seawalls designed to protect them. The point is tipped with a long spit, visible at low tide, formed by longshore sediments that move south along the outer shore. On the inner shore, sediment moves to the north. A broad sandy area visible from the ferry appears free of bulkheads. Actually, this is a small foreland that partially encircles a tiny brackish lagoon. The lagoon itself has been deepened and widened with a small channel that opens onto Eagle Harbor—a convenient "harbor" for the upland owner.

To the west is a large creosote piling- and timber-treating plant. So long has this operation been a fixture of Eagle Harbor that the locality goes by the name "Creosote." The treating plant is situated on fill. Old pilings mark the plant's former loading pier. West of Creosote, the shore curves gently beneath the community of Eagledale. A boat haven is located on the waterfront.

Eagle Harbor

Eagle Harbor illustrates one of the great ironies of life on Puget Sound. Its proximity to downtown Seattle via ferry has transformed this once-sleepy farming and shipbuilding community into a bustling suburbia. Boasting very expensive amenities typical of the best of Puget Sound, the community is nevertheless situated on one of the Sound's most polluted waterways. Industry-caused sediment contamination has accumulated for generations—most of it predating environmental laws. The disturbing result is a natural environment characterized by a relatively low quantity of fish and shellfish. Because of very high levels of pre-tumorous and tumorous conditions in bottomfish of Eagle Harbor's contaminated sediments, fishing is not advised. Clams and crabs harvested in Eagle Harbor also are considered unfit for human consumption. Yet the signs of robust relationship between people and their natural environment abound here. An educated populace and a beautiful setting add up to the best possible relationship between Puget Sound and people.

As the ferry moves toward its berth, the Washington State Ferry shipyard lies west of the ferry terminal, with a marina beyond. Condominiums line the shore between the ferry terminal and the shipyard. East of the ferry terminal, a high bluff towers over the pebble beach. Several hundred yards down the beach, the backshore levels out into a lowland. The broad beach here fronts the lowland area, once a salt marsh.

Great blue herons, kingfishers, pigeons, gulls, starlings and other waterfront birds are common at the ferry dock. During the winter, look for grebes, loons and other divers and dabblers.

EDMONDS/ KINGSTON

The Edmonds-to-Kingston ferry crosses the main basin of Puget Sound about 15 miles north of Seattle. Here, the Sound narrows into a single channel about 4 miles wide. Just south of the ferry route is Puget Sound's deepest point (more than 900 feet). To the north, the Sound branches around Whidbey Island. The ferry route angles across the Sound toward the southwest and ends in Appletree Cove, the site of the town of Kingston. The crossing takes about 24 minutes.

Edmonds

The city of Edmonds was incorporated in 1890. Its name is apparently a misspelling of Edmund, the name Wilkes gave, in 1841, to the point on which the town is situated. In another account, Edmonds received its name in honor of Vermont's famous U.S. Senator George Franklin Edmonds.

The Edmonds ferry terminal is about one mile north of Point Edwards (also a corruption of Edmund) and just south of the entrance to Possession Sound.

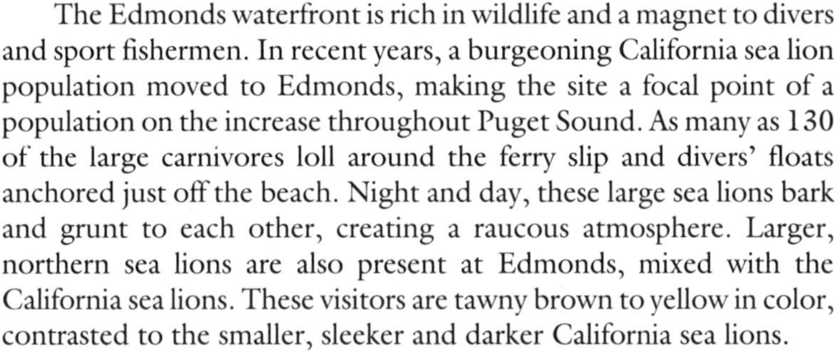

The Edmonds waterfront is rich in wildlife and a magnet to divers and sport fishermen. In recent years, a burgeoning California sea lion population moved to Edmonds, making the site a focal point of a population on the increase throughout Puget Sound. As many as 130 of the large carnivores loll around the ferry slip and divers' floats anchored just off the beach. Night and day, these large sea lions bark and grunt to each other, creating a raucous atmosphere. Larger, northern sea lions are also present at Edmonds, mixed with the California sea lions. These visitors are tawny brown to yellow in color, contrasted to the smaller, sleeker and darker California sea lions.

Edmonds' sea lions are seasonal visitors. The California sea lions are all males, part of a population of 4,000 to 5,000 that migrates to Washington and British Columbia from the breeding grounds in the Channel Islands off Southern California. Of these, about 900 to 1,200 move into Puget Sound in late September, staying until about May. Typically, they congregate in areas near isolated haulout sites, such as floats, abandoned barges and buoys. At Edmonds, they congregate on the divers' floats and on the floating guide pier of the ferry slip. At times they have been numerous enough on the guide pier to cause a serious list in the floating structure; today a fence along its northern edge prevents the overload of sea lions. During the peak of the sea lions' visit, ferry travelers often complain of the overpowering smell of sea lion waste on the pier.

Underwater, the shallow water off Edmonds is a rich habitat for marine life. Originally, the bottom consisted of flat, compact sand and gravel. Decades of log storage for a now-defunct sawmill added considerable woody debris to the bottom. Over the years, several artificial reefs—including a sunken dry dock and pontoons for a replica of the Hood Canal floating bridge—have been set on the bottom as a way of increasing the diversity of fishes and invertebrates. A dry dock sits just north of the ferry dock, where the water depth is between 40 and 50 feet. The dry dock is 325 feet long, with side walls that rise 34 feet above its inner deck, creating two long walls covered with attached sea anemones and tubeworms. Known to divers as the Edmonds Underwater Park, the area is rich with fishes like rockfish, greenling, lingcod and flounder. Because of its proximity to the large urban population of northern King County, its spectacular marine life and its relatively easy dive conditions, many divers are trained here.

South of the ferry dock, an array of other artificial reefs was established to create diverse habitats and increase the abundance of fish near the public fishing pier. Tires, banded together to form pyramids and other shapes, were placed on the bottom in the late 1970s. Studies conducted on the reefs found that structures that

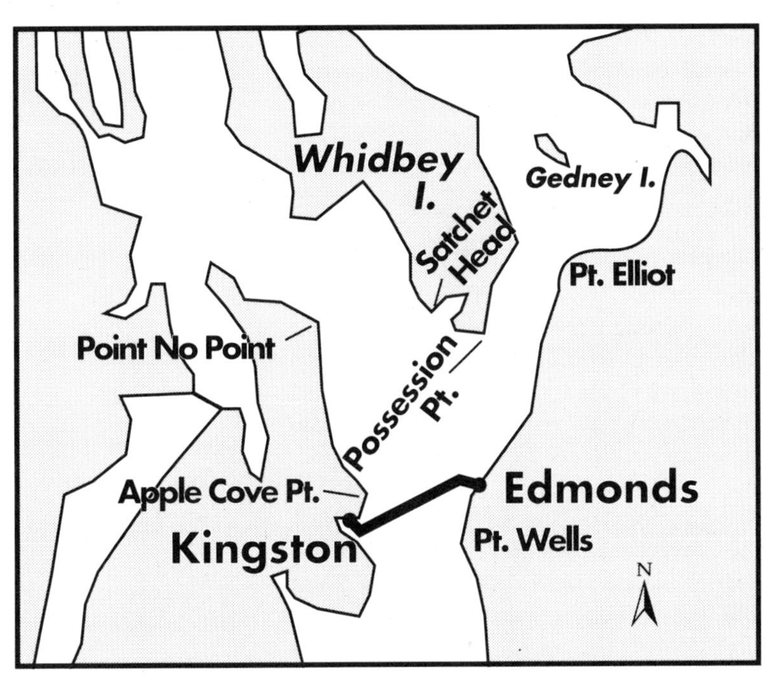

created greater relief attracted the most fish. Even the numbers of bottom-dwelling fish, such as flounder and sole, which usually thrive on a flat bottom, increased with the addition of more habitat variety. The reefs are marked with small orange and white buoys just offshore of the fishing pier.

The Edmonds waterfront is a mix of structures. North of the ferry dock, the shoreline consists of rip-rap armor placed along the mainline railroad tracks. Bracketts Landing Beach is next to the ferry dock to the north. Old pilings, left over from lumber days, and a large rock pile create some habitat diversity in the intertidal zone. South of the ferry dock, a narrow beach runs for several hundred yards. The rip-rap jetty that encloses the boat haven lies immediately beyond. The Edmonds fishing pier is the concrete walkway built along the marina jetty. This is a very popular spot for shore anglers seeking perch, cod, flounder, sole and occasional salmon.

As the ferry pulls away from Edmonds, it turns south into the channel. Edwards Point is the hillside south of downtown, with a prominent cluster of oil storage tanks. The oil loading dock is located south of the Edmonds marina. Point Wells is farther south. It too has an oil-loading facility; its squat storage tanks are right on the cuspate foreland of the waterfront.

As the ferry enters the channel, you can see up and down the Sound for a considerable distance. To the north is Whidbey Island, splitting the Sound into two channels. The channel to the northeast is Possession Sound, which leads toward Everett and Port Gardner. Ferries of the Clinton-Mukilteo route are visible as they ply the water between the mainland and Whidbey Island.

The point of land visible farthest along the eastern shore is Point Elliot. Beyond, in the distance, are bluffs between Priest Point and Tulalip, northwest of Everett. Possession Point is the more easterly of the two headlands at Whidbey Island's southern tip. Scatchet Head forms the western bluff separating Possession Sound from Admiralty Inlet (the main channel leading toward the Strait of Juan de Fuca). The two headlands are separated by Cultus Bay, named from the Chinook Jargon word for "worthless," apparently because it is so shallow. The

western shore of Whidbey Island forms a great arc enclosing Useless Bay. Useless is bordered on the north by a steep bluff, visible especially when the sunlight is low and from the east. This bluff is composed of soft debris of the Whidbey formation, water-laid deposits of sand, clay and fine gravel from a period between glacial advances about 100,000 to 150,000 years ago. Admiralty Inlet actually makes a dog-leg to the west around Double Bluff, the point of land on the left-hand end of the soft cliff. Point-No-Point is the low promontory along the western shore of the Sound. Look for its cluster of white buildings.

To the south, Mount Rainier is visible in clear weather, towering over the dark lowlands. Look for the skyline of downtown Seattle peeking over the low saddle along the distant southeastern shore. Magnolia and West Point are the most distant forms on the eastern shore.

The western shore consists of Bainbridge Island in the distance to the south. The broad inlet of Port Madison separates Bainbridge Island from Point Jefferson. The deepest part of the Sound occurs just off Point Jefferson: soundings near mid-channel exceed 900 feet in places. President Point is just north of Point Jefferson and forms what appears to be the southern promontory enclosing Appletree Cove.

Wildlife of the Sound's central channel consists of transient marine mammals, including Minke whales, gray whales, harbor porpoises, Dall's porpoises and sea lions. Because of the undulating shore that lines the Sound along both sides, eddies can form on the ebb and flood, when currents are running the hardest. One secret to wildlife sightings in the central basin is to watch for such eddies. Herring and other small fish tend to shoal in these convergence zones, attracting the entire range of predators, from noisily foraging gulls to feeding whales.

About 12 minutes out of Edmonds, the ferry sits in mid-channel, approaching Appletree Cove. Just north of the cove is Apple Cove Point, a high bluff covered with mixed hardwoods (alders and maples) and fringed by a few weather-torn firs. Apple Cove Point has a low sandspit at its base, now developed with residences. Converging currents along the shore built this deposit. Evidence of landslides is apparent on the bluff south of Apple Cove Point—the source for some of the material that comprises the low spit on Apple Cove Point. Material along the top of the bluff consists of Vashon till, laid and compressed during the last glacial advance into the Puget lowlands. Several exposed cliff faces reveal distinct bedding layers. This material predates the Vashon till and consists of sand and clay laid down in a large body of water that was formed as the glacier moved southward. These deposits are known as Esperance sand.

Appletree Cove

Appletree Cove earned its name from "wild apples" seen growing in the area by Lt. Charles Wilkes. Although wild crabapples are native to the region, some believe Wilkes actually saw blooming dogwood trees. Apple Cove Point inherited its name because of its proximity to the cove. As the boat nears land, look for eagles perching in the firs along the bluff. Other seabirds that frequent the cove's calmer water include gulls, grebes, dabbling ducks, loons and diving birds. During the summer, look for rhinoceros auklets and arctic terns.

Not far offshore from the ferry dock, the boat passes over a bank that extends southeastward from Apple Cove Point. The deeper trough of the cove drops off to the southeast and is an extension of the lowland depression behind Appletree Cove. This spur canyon leads off into the Puget Sound abyss.

The ferry dock at Kingston extends considerably out into the water. Just south of the ferry terminal, a large breakwater encloses a marina. The rip-rap bank of the breakwater is basalt, common west of Puget Sound (rip-rap along the eastern shore of the Sound is primarily sandstone, native to the Cascades). Aside from the conspicuous alteration of the shoreline near the ferry terminal and marina, Appletree Cove still possesses a natural quality; beaches ring the cove and uplands are developed into a spacious, if suburban, residential environment. Although Kingston was incorporated in 1888, Appletree Cove was the site of one of the earliest sawmills on Puget Sound. In 1853, it was one of a handful of sites on the Sound where opportunistic easterners began taking the timber that reached tidewater edge.

MUKILTEO/ CLINTON

The 15-minute ferry crossing that links Mukilteo with Clinton on Whidbey Island introduces us to Possession Sound, the southern entrance to the Whidbey Basin of Puget Sound. The Whidbey Basin extends northward past the tip of the island, connecting with Padilla Bay by way of the Swinomish Slough and the Strait of Juan de Fuca through Deception Pass. The Whidbey Basin is unique in that it receives the runoff of three very large river systems: the Skagit, the Stillaguamish and the Snohomish. The chemical effects of this fresh-water runoff are particularly evident in Possession Sound, where surface water is much less salty than in more open parts of the Sound.

Vancouver named Possession Sound and Possession Point to commemorate his formal act of possessing New Georgia and the shores lining the inland sea of what is now Puget Sound. On June 4, 1792 at Mission Beach, on the northeastern shore of the Sound, he solemnly enacted the ceremony, claiming the land for Great Britain.

Possession Point marks the southern end of Whidbey Island. The point absorbs the punishing waves generated in the long fetch of Puget Sound's central basin. An extensive bank forms a shallow ledge south of the point and attracts fleets of sport fishermen and marine wildlife.

Mukilteo

The ferry dock in Mukilteo is actually on Point Elliot, named by Lt. Charles Wilkes during his 1838-1842 exploration in honor of Midshipman Samuel Elliott. Vancouver had anchored just a few hundred yards offshore on May 30, 1792. Point Elliot was the site of the 1855 signing of the Treaty of Point Elliott (one "t" has been dropped in modern usage), in which northern Puget Sound Indians ceded their lands and retained their traditional fishing and hunting rights.

The Mukilteo lighthouse, which began operation in 1906, now is dwarfed by a large shorefront apartment building. The beach and upland area south of the lighthouse grounds is Mukilteo State Park, a day-use area with a boat launch.

Point Elliot is lined by a steep pebble/cobble beach. The large flat area that comprises the lowland between the water and the railroad tracks originally was enclosed by a long spit formed by longshore currents from the south. At the time of Vancouver's visit the flat ground of the point was covered with wild roses in bloom. Just offshore is a shallow ledge; beyond that the bottom drops off quickly.

At the point where the ferry crosses Possession Sound the water reaches depths of more than 500 feet.

As the ferry pulls away from Mukilteo look north into Possession Sound. Visible in the middle distance is Gedney Island (known locally as Hat Island). Beyond Gedney Island and to the west is Camano Head, the steep southern tip of Camano Island. The waterway separating Camano Island from the mainland on the right is Port Susan, a long, shallow inlet fed by the Stillaguamish River. Saratoga Passage separates Camano Island from Whidbey Island. The mighty Skagit River flows into Puget Sound about 25 miles north.

Port Gardner

Visible to the east is Port Gardner and the city of Everett, marked by the plume of its paper mill. The lowland just north of Everett is the mouth of the Snohomish River. If you use binoculars, you can see Jetty Island lining the Everett waterfront. Jetty Island was created in the early 1900s. Two long lines of pilings were driven parallel to the shore, then filled with large boulders to form a breakwater. Over the years, sediment from the Snohomish River has been deposited on the island. It is now an important haulout site for harbor seals and California and northern sea lions, and a nesting site for Arctic terns and glaucous-winged gulls. Offshore are extensive eelgrass beds. The City of Everett operates naturalist programs on the island during summer months.

Across the Snohomish River mouth from Everett are Priest Point and Mission Beach on the Tulalip Indian Reservation. Although the shore features are not visible from the ferry because of the distance, notice the direction of waves moving toward Mission Beach. Because it lies perpendicular to the fetch of Possession Sound, waves hit

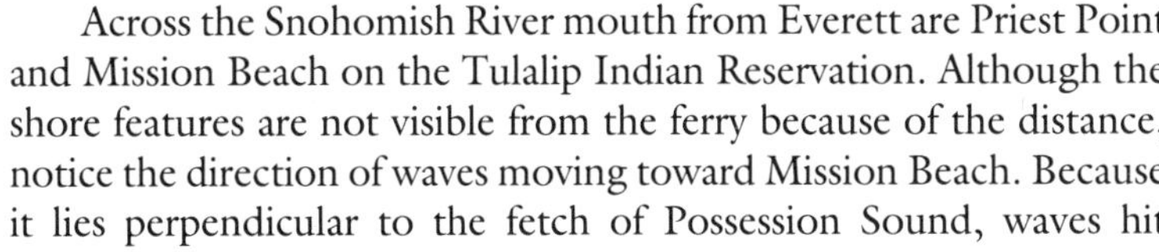

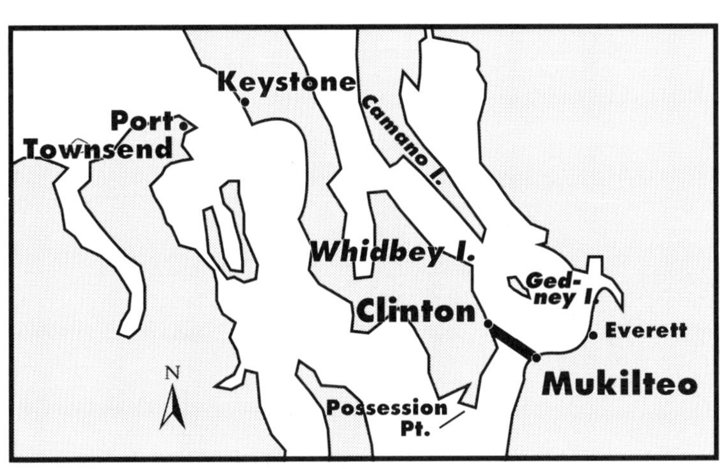

squarely; longshore currents move away from its center and have built feathery spits on either end.

Gedney Island is probably the remnant tip of Camano Island; contour charts of the bottom show a prominent ridge or sill connecting them. As delta sediments continue to be deposited by the Snohomish River, the passage leading into Port Susan east of Gedney Island will become shallower, further isolating Port Susan as a distinct body of water.

Camano Head is the landslide-scarred prow of land northwest of Gedney Island. It was named for the island, which in 1790 had been named for Lt. Cmdr. Jacinto Caamaño of the Spanish navy, by Francisco de Eliza. Camano Island extends north about 15 miles and is separated from the mainland only by narrow Davis Slough in the vicinity of the Stillaguamish River mouth.

Whidbey Island

West of the ferry is Whidbey Island. Thirty-eight-mile-long Whidbey Island is the second-largest island in the lower 48 states (Long Island, New York is the largest). It was named by Vancouver in honor of Joseph Whidbey, master of the *Discovery.* Whidbey probed Deception Pass, at the island's northern end, and established its separation from the mainland.

The broad beach that faces Possession Sound is known as Columbia Beach. It is maintained by steady longshore currents that bring sediments northward from Possession Point. Extensive eelgrass beds line Columbia Beach, home to a host of marine invertebrates and nearshore fishes.

The wildlife of Possession Sound is varied. Terns, gulls, cormorants and diving birds are common because of the high productivity in the converging currents and nearby nesting colonies. Minke whales and Dall's porpoises are commonly seen near Possession Point. Large herds of California sea lions inhabit the area, as well as northern sea lions and harbor seals. Eagles are common along the shores of the sound and on Gedney Island.

KEYSTONE/ PORT TOWNSEND

The 35-minute ferry ride between Keystone and Port Townsend can be one of Puget Sound's most adventurous crossings. High winds and ocean swells penetrate the Strait of Juan de Fuca and frequently cause delays. During any season, but particularly in winter, conditions can arise that make for a lively ride. For naturalists, abundant wildlife, particularly seabirds from nearby breeding and feeding grounds, provide opportunities to see large numbers of alcids (diving birds) and gulls. The fact that the wild Pacific is close at hand is shown by the forces at work and the animals seen on this route.

As the major crossing point between the North Cascades and the Olympic Peninsula, the ferry often is choked with traffic during the summer. But you can take advantage of the delays and enjoy birding and beach strolling near the Keystone dock and in Port Townsend.

The Port Townsend-Keystone ferry crosses Admiralty Inlet, the neck of water that connects the Strait of Juan de Fuca with the Central Basin of Puget Sound. The entrance is defined as an imaginary line between Point Wilson at the tip of the Quimper Peninsula, and Partridge Point on Whidbey Island. Captain Vancouver named the feature in the spring of 1792 when he saw the opening to the south of the "dead end" of the Strait of Juan de Fuca. At 38 miles in length, Whidbey Island is the second largest island in the contiguous United States (overshadowed by New York's Long Island).

Keystone Harbor

The narrow cleft tucked beneath the southern end of the bluff of Admiralty Head is Keystone Harbor. The ferry passes seemingly too close to the cobble beach—but fear not, the dropoff is steep and, in all but the lowest tides, the ferry has plenty of water (runs *are* interrupted for the lowest tides—usually in June). Keystone Harbor is enclosed by a jetty, constructed along its south edge. As is often the case where shores are altered to suit man's purposes, the seawall has changed the natural regime of sediment transport along the shore. Scouring has occurred south of the jetty and the beach has eroded dozens of yards inland. The harbor itself serves as a sediment trap and must be dredged periodically. Perhaps some degree of tradeoff has been achieved, however, with the creation of reef habitat along the submerged portion of the jetty. Keystone jetty is a very popular site for recreational scuba divers and is one of Washington's most popular underwater marine sanctuaries. Lingcod, rockfish, kelp greenling and schools of sand lance and herring commonly are seen by divers amid the boulders, along with a host of invertebrates including sea urchins, featherduster worms, sea cucumbers and giant barnacles.

As the ferry passes close to the jetty at Keystone, look carefully among the boulders for black oystercatchers. These birds have distinctive long red bills and red legs. In spite of their name, oystercatchers do not prey on oysters, preferring instead mussels, limpets and barnacles exposed on the rocks at low tide. With long, chisel-like bills, they pry open shells and eat the succulent contents.

Landward of the ferry dock is a large freshwater lagoon known as Crocket Lake, separated from Admiralty Bay by a long strand of driftlog-strewn beach. This beach is a strong indicator of a depositional shore; in the budget of sediments along the shore, it is a net recipient. High bluffs to the south are the source of some of the fine particles carried northward by the strong currents of Admiralty Bay, the broad expanse of water to the southeast.

Southeast of the ferry dock, pigeon guillemots nest on an abandoned pier a short distance off the beach. Kingfishers, great blue herons and bald eagles are common.

Within a few minutes of leaving Keystone Harbor, the ferry enters a great tide-rip off Admiralty Head. As tidal movement on the flood

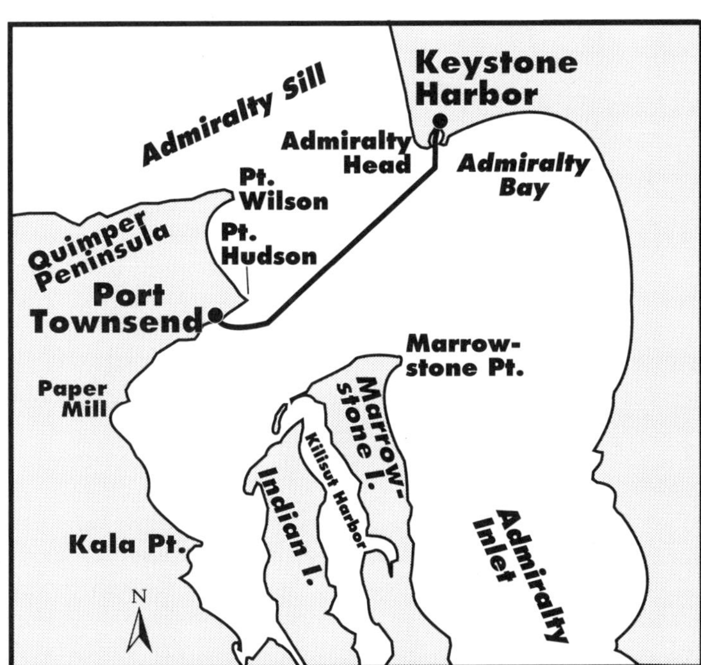

or ebb builds, a vast eddy forms in Admiralty Bay, with the opposing currents converging just off the shore below Fort Casey State Park. On a flood tide, water rushes over the Admiralty Sill southward and forms a great gyre, or circular sweep, east and northward along the low shore of Admiralty Bay. As it circles northward it collides with the rush of incoming water just off the point in a welter of pyramid-shaped waves and restless chatter. The rip is visible for a great distance as a distinct change of texture on the sea's surface. The even swells moving from the northwest appear to break against the rip. You may even notice a new roll in the motion of the boat as you pass into the convergence zone. Although the turbulence is a bit rough for large rafts of birds, the area is very productive of forage fish. Scattered gulls, auklets, pigeon guillemots and murres feed here.

Center channel

Visible from the route, the San Juan Islands rise distantly to the north, with Smith Island light blinking in the middle distance. To the west, Port Townsend's picturesque buildings cling to the hillside near the eastern tip of Quimper Peninsula. South, across Port Townsend Bay, are Indian and Marrowstone Islands, separated by the narrow inlet of Kilsut Harbor. In clear weather, the ferry vantage allows views of both the North Cascades rising above the lowland to the east, and the Olympics towering beyond the foothills to the west. This view of the Olympics is essentially a look at the northeastern corner of the range. The eastern front lines the horizon to the south; the jagged summits of the northeastern corner of the range appear to the west.

Many of the shorelines visible along this route are high, tan-colored bluffs. These cliffs consist of sand, gravel and clay deposited by several episodes of glaciation during the Pleistocene epoch. Easily eroded by waves breaking along the beach, these bluffs are a significant source of sediment that moves along the shore via longshore transport. As waves break against the slope "toe," they continuously undermine the unconsolidated material in the bluff and form narrow, steep cobble beaches along the water. Notice the orientation of the bluffs. Many are located on shores where wave action is intense, due to the long fetch, or distances of open water where waves form. The broad beaches along Whidbey Island's western shore, and the low spits that form the tips of major points in the vicinity, have been created from material eroded from the weathering bluffs.

During any month of the year, but especially during the summer, be on the lookout for orca whales, which cruise through Admiralty Inlet following the great schools of salmon returning to the rivers. Orcas commonly travel in small pods of four to eight animals and can be seen far away as they rhythmically cut through the water. Dall's porpoises are often seen off Admiralty Head, traveling in pods of five to 10. Because of the porpoises' black-and-white markings, excited viewers frequently mistake them for orcas. These little cetaceans are only four to six feet in length, however, not the 20 to 30 feet of mature orcas. Look for Dall's porpoises alongside the ferry, playing the bow wake at top speed.

Solitary pilot whales have been seen along the route. Pilot whales also are occasionally confused with orcas; their distinguishing features are low, crescent-shaped dorsal fins and blunt heads.

The proximity to harbor seal haulout sites at Protection Island and Smith Island national wildlife refuges assures healthy harbor seal populations. Harbor seal sightings are common; look for seals' heads poking out of the water, the smooth, gray form staring expressionless with dark eyes. California sea lions have been observed on the run, but sightings are rare.

Admiralty Sill

Although a visual sweep of the northern horizon gives you an expansive view toward the San Juan Islands, one of Puget Sound's most significant bathymetric features lies in that direction but is invisible from the water's surface. Just north of the ferry route, the bottom rises sharply, creating a threshold known as the Admiralty Sill, which separates the deeper Strait of Juan de Fuca from Puget Sound. The depth of the sill varies from about 120 to 240 feet. It defines the northern rim of the Puget Sound Basin, and its influence on the rate of exchange between Puget Sound water and Pacific seawater is profound.

Because of the sill's restricting influence, and the fact that water parcels of different temperature and salinity occupy distinct strata in the water column, water circles vertically within the basin, driven by movement of the tide. Cold water enters on an incoming tide and falls over the sill into the basin's depths. Elsewhere in the basin, freshwater enters from rivers and moves along the surface. The overall effect of these movements is the creation of a grand, but very slow, cycling process. Very little water actually enters or leaves the basin on any given tide, and full exchange can require many months. Freshwater flowing into the southern Puget Sound Basin may require months of cycling through the maze of channels before finally being drawn over the Admiralty Sill and out to sea on ebb tide. Similarly, sediments—whether they consist of silt washing into the Sound from the mountains, or urban contaminants entering through storm drains—tend to settle within the basin rather than be swept to the ocean.

A sill is an area of considerable turbulence within the water column. In an estuary like Puget Sound, huge quantities of freshwater are added constantly by the region's rivers. Freshwater tends to "float" over saltier water, drawing some saltwater along with it. As the water moves over a sill, water drawn from depths mixes with surface water. Although the sill restricts the movement of water in and out of the basin, the water that does move over the sill is well blended by the turbulence.

Midchannel Bank

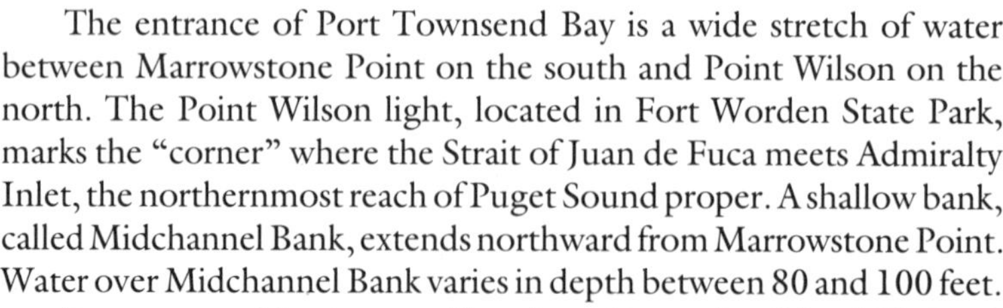

The entrance of Port Townsend Bay is a wide stretch of water between Marrowstone Point on the south and Point Wilson on the north. The Point Wilson light, located in Fort Worden State Park, marks the "corner" where the Strait of Juan de Fuca meets Admiralty Inlet, the northernmost reach of Puget Sound proper. A shallow bank, called Midchannel Bank, extends northward from Marrowstone Point. Water over Midchannel Bank varies in depth between 80 and 100 feet.

In summer, rhinoceros auklets from Protection Island National Wildlife Refuge travel to Midchannel Bank. They forage for fish by day and return at dusk to their nest burrows on the sparsely populated island located north of the mouth of Discovery Bay. The chunky bird is easily recognized by a small horn on its yellowish bill, two prominent white plumes on the face, and by its strong flight, low over the water. The rhinoceros auklets gather over shallow banks at the entrance to Port Townsend Bay and just off the point of Admiralty Head, often mixed with large flocks of glaucous-winged and Heerman's gulls.

Also common are pigeon guillemots—black birds about the size and shape of a common pigeon. Their white wing bars and bright red feet are visible as they take flight from the water. Watch carefully for the clown-like tufted puffin, with its oversized orange beak and long white tufts over the eyes. Although not commonly seen, small breeding populations are present in this part of Puget Sound. Like the auklets, they feed over a broad area during the long summer days.

During summer months look for dense congregations of glaucous-winged gulls feeding in a frenzied manner. They indicate the presence of large schools of forage fish, such as herring and sand lance. Herring respond to predators by gathering into dense balls—thousands of fish literally packed into a sphere as each tries to nose to the center of the mass to avoid predators. Gulls are almost always present, but herring balls are frequently attacked simultaneously by dogfish and other predators underwater too.

During the winter, the cast of characters among the seabirds changes dramatically. Those commonly seen along the Port Townsend-Keystone run include gulls, murres, grebes and loons.

Port Townsend Bay

Southwest of Point Wilson, the beach curves gently to Point Hudson, located at the east end of Water Street, Port Townsend's downtown thoroughfare. Prior to development of Port Townsend, Point Hudson was a long tongue of sand and cobble. This beach was an important village and trading place for the Klallam people, whose territory encompassed the Strait of Juan de Fuca from the Hoko River eastward to a point near the entrance to Hood Canal. Most of what is now downtown Port Townsend is built on fill. The street-level terrace running along the waterfront was carved into the pale bluff to provide shore access along what was originally a steep cobble beach. Although much of the downtown shore consists of seawall, small pocket beaches are scattered along the waterfront, lined with sand during the summer and cobble rocks during the winter. Piers along the waterfront are rich habitat for pile perch, shiner perch, sea anemones, mussels and tubeworms.

In addition to its well known historical ambience, Port Townsend offers the naturalist some pleasant side-trips. Fort Worden, about two miles from the ferry terminal, is good for birders and botanists. Dune plant communities are found on Point Wilson. The Port Townsend Marine Science Center, located at Fort Worden, has live exhibits of marine fishes and invertebrates. A little-known enclave of native prairie wildflowers is found in a corner of the municipal golf course, located about $1^1/_2$ miles northwest of the ferry terminal. Camas and several other plants, now rare in the northern Puget Lowland, have been preserved on this small plot of city land.

Port Townsend is a major port of entry for travelers bound for Olympic National Park and the outer Olympic Coast. This ferry run offers the first chance to "stretch your legs" en route to the pristine natural environments of the Olympic Peninsula. But don't leave your binoculars in the car—this ferry ride is a fitting introduction to a naturalist's paradise.

GUEMES ISLAND

The Guemes Island ferry is one of Puget Sound's shortest runs, yet on it we see, in miniature, the mix of industry, natural forces and natural resources that characterizes the whole Puget Sound environment. Oil tanker traffic, the nearby Padilla Bay estuary, commercial fishing vessels, salmon and seabirds, recreational boaters and the combination of an urban setting (Anacortes) and a rural community (Guemes Island) all are clustered around this narrow channel off Rosario Strait. This mix draws both the potential conflicts and common interest of all the users into focus. And on several occasions, mishaps involving the marine transport of oil have brought this area into the news, livening the debate on our priorities for Puget Sound.

Guemes Channel is a narrow passage between Guemes Island on the north and Fidalgo Island on the south. The channel runs about three miles in length and connects Rosario Strait with Padilla Bay. Thankfully, "Guemes" is a shortened version of the name of the person whom Guemes Island and channel honor. The explorer Lt. Juan Francisco de Eliza named Guemes Island to show his respect for the Viceroy of Mexico—Señor Don Juan Vincente de Guemes Pacheco y Padillo Orcasitas y Aguayo, Conde de Revilla Gigedo. Other parts of this name appear scattered across the map as Orcas Island and Padilla Bay.

At its west end are Shannon Point, a rocky promontory on Fidalgo Island and Kelly Point, the bluff on Guemes Island. Cypress Island is the high, rocky landform to the northwest. In the distance, James, Decatur, Lopez, Blakely and San Juan islands line the horizon on the western side of Rosario Strait. To the east, Mt. Baker is visible through the channel; Hat Island sits off the steep bluff of Guemes Island's eastern tip. The city of Anacortes occupies the south bank.

The ferry crossing is brief—five to 10 minutes. Notice, however, an unusual adaptation with the 22-car ferryboat. Because of currents that sometimes exceed five knots, the boat is equipped with an outdrive propulsion system, enabling it to turn its propellers into the current and move sideways, if necessary, to cross the surging channel. This channel has formidable currents because it forms the funnel through which a large part of the water from Padilla Bay must pour. The Padilla Bay Estuary covers about 15,000 acres in a large embayment to the east. On the average tide change, 75,000 acre-feet of water move in or out of Padilla Bay. Although some of the water moves through Swinomish Slough and around the east of Guemes Island, much of it races through the narrow pass.

Guemes differs from its neighbor islands in geologic composition. This is evident in its flatness. While most of the San Juans and Fidalgo Island are composed of very old rocks (between about 600 million and 30 million years old), Guemes consists mainly of glacial debris about 12,000 years old. While the older rocks resisted the ice's erosive action, Guemes is a product of glacial deposition. Only its southeastern tip contains bedrock of the pre-glacial landscape. The shores of Guemes Channel reveal the current's effect on the soft material. Currents have eroded bluffs in the eastern part of the channel and transported sediments along the shore to a broad beach on Guemes Island just west of the ferry landing. Here is an outstanding example of the relationship between a source and a destination of sediments moved by longshore currents—only a short distance separates the site of erosion from the site of deposition.

Eelgrass beds are found on the southern shore of the channel. Although important here, they pale in size next to the vast submerged meadows of Padilla Bay. There, more than 10,000 acres of eelgrass habitat are protected within the Padilla Bay National Estuarine Sanctuary. (A visit to the Breazeale Interpretive Center at Bayview is strongly recommended.)

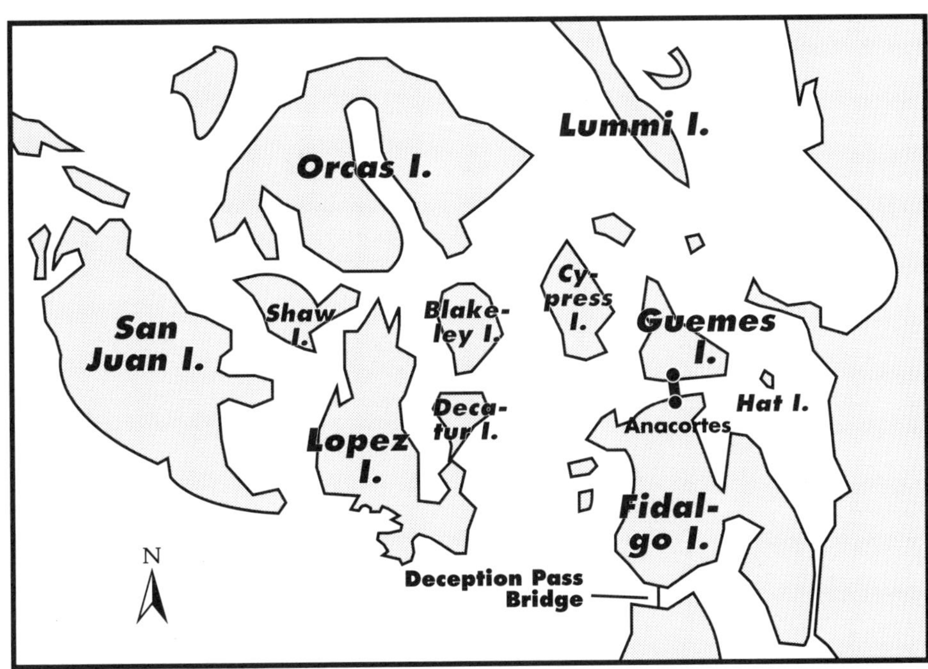

Wildlife of Guemes Channel includes gulls, cormorants and grebes. Forage fish move along the shallows of the channel edge; birds work the current's eddies searching for prey. Pigeon guillemots nest along the channel in spring; bald eagles also nest in the vicinity. Nearby Padilla Bay hosts large colonies of nesting glaucous-winged gulls and large flocks of shorebirds and waders. Migratory waterfowl are particularly abundant here—marshes and fields of the Skagit Valley teem with ducks, geese and swans during the fall and spring migrations. Few sights are as memorable as a twilight sky filled with lacy skeins of northering geese.

River otters are common in Guemes Channel, most often seen to the west of the ferry route. Pilot whales have been seen in the channel; both harbor and Dall's porpoises frequent nearby areas. Harbor seals haul out on the southeastern point of Guemes and are common in the channel.

Along with commercial fishing boats, expect to see oil tankers negotiating this narrow waterway. March Point, hidden from view by the town of Anacortes, lies to the southeast. Several oil refineries receive and ship petroleum products from March Point docks. Two famous mishaps have occurred here. In 1971, a tanker ran aground, spilling oil. Another spill occurred in January 1988, when an oil barge flipped over and sank just off Shannon Point. Its cargo consisted mostly of very heavy oil that sank after escaping from the broken vessel. Investigations later found traces of the heavy sludge in Guemes Channel and parts of Padilla Bay. This damage was not visible; only time will reveal the extent of its impact on the marine environment.

Both events raise obvious questions about marine safety and environmental risk. What they alert us to, also, is the larger question of how our society reconciles technology and material needs to environmental protection. Puget Sound, the natural treasure we all cherish, is also a resource of transportation and commerce. Where do we draw the lines?

LUMMI ISLAND

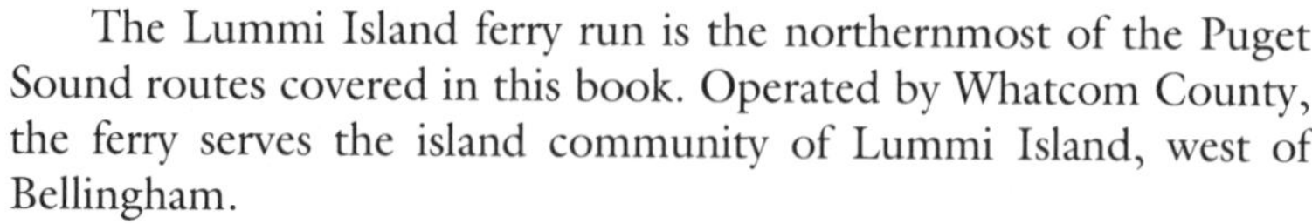

The Lummi Island ferry run is the northernmost of the Puget Sound routes covered in this book. Operated by Whatcom County, the ferry serves the island community of Lummi Island, west of Bellingham.

The ride is short, but its brevity offset by outstanding scenery and the exceptional exploring opportunity that a trip to Lummi Island offers.

The ferry route crosses Hale Passage, a three-quarter-mile-wide channel on Lummi's northeastern side. Hale Passage connects Lummi Bay and Bellingham Bay and is named for Horatio Hale, the linguist who accompanied the Wilkes Expedition on its round-the-world exploration between 1838 and 1842. Hale distinguished himself during that voyage by collecting the vocabulary of the Chinook Jargon, the trade language of Northwest Coast Indians. Hale's dictionaries were the principal phrase books used throughout the Northwest for communication between Indians and white settlers. Many Chinook words are with us today, on maps and in regional usage. "Skookum," for example, means "strong, stout or large." Skookum Inlet in the South Sound bears reference to its large size. Several ferryboats in the Washington State ferry fleet also bear Chinook names, including *Tillicum,* meaning "friend," and *Klahowya,* meaning "welcome."

Hale himself is honored twice in Puget Sound geography—both times with passages. Hale Passage is also the name of the narrow body of water separating Fox Island and Point Fosdick, just south of the Tacoma Narrows.

The mainland ferry dock is on Gooseberry Point, a low windswept foreland crowded with cottages. Currents in the pass move swiftly, and high winter tides occasionally toss debris onto the beach. To the west of the ferry dock is an unusual marina. Boats are stored on land and moved in and out of the water by an overhead tram. Just east of the ferry dock is the Lummi Nation fish processing plant operated by the Lummi Tribe. The beach here is sandy, grading to gravel to the east. Longshore currents move mostly to the west on the Gooseberry Point side and east on the island side. The pass shallows to a sandy bar on its western end.

Look for Dungeness crabs and small fish on the sandy bottom below the Gooseberry Point dock. In springtime, the pass is an

important spawning ground for herring and, during the winter, large schools of herring congregate here.

As the ferry pulls away from the dock, notice the towering form of Lummi Peak, 1,600 feet above sea level. Its steep sides have all but precluded development on the southern end of the island. Lummi's north end, in contrast, is gentle rolling terrain and has been farmed and settled. Visible to the southeast is distant Eliza Island. Its Spanish pronunciation ("ay-LEES-a") long ago gave way to current usage, which makes the "i" long and hardens the "z." Wilkes named the island for the Spanish navigator Juan Francisco de Eliza, who preceded Vancouver in exploration of the Strait of Juan de Fuca and the San Juan Islands.

Along the eastern shore of Hale Passage, Portage Island is connected to the mainland by a broad cobble causeway visible at low tides. At high tide, the island is separated from the mainland by the shallow channel. The island and the connecting spit are part of the Lummi Reservation.

North of the ferry route, Lummi Point juts out from Lummi Island. In the distance across Lummi Bay is Sandy Point. As its name suggests, Sandy Point consists of fine sediments, carried southward along the eastern shore of the Strait of Georgia after being eroded from the bluffs near Cherry Point.

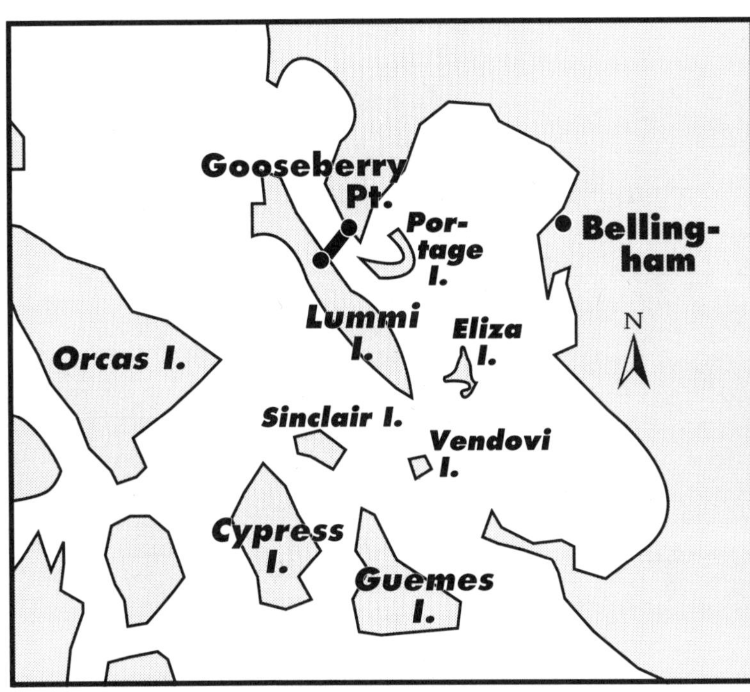

As the ferry approaches the Lummi island dock, notice the outcrops of rock near the ferry landing. These sedimentary rocks are between 36 million and 60 million years old and very similar in age and composition to the sandstone of the Chuckanut Mountains, visible in the distance beyond Eliza Island. Those rocks in the intertidal zone host large colonies of fucus, or rockweed, a kelp with twin-lobed air sacs.

Once ashore on Lummi Island, visit the island's west side. From Village Point, enjoy spectacular views of Orcas Island. The reef-net salmon fishery is in full swing during the summer months. This technique originated here and in the San Juan Islands among the Lummi Indians, whose summer fishing villages were scattered throughout the islands. In this technique, a large net is stretched out between two boats simulating a rising bottom or reef. Salmon follow the surface of the net upward and are funneled into a trap net. This prehistoric method remains a very effective method for taking large numbers of the salmon that flood through the narrow passages and over the reefs of the San Juan Islands en route to the Fraser River.

Wildlife of Hale Passage includes great blue herons, bald eagles, kingfishers and scoters, grebes, gulls and cormorants. Pigeon guillemots nest in the vicinity. Migrating terns and jaegers are occasionally seen during summer months. Harbor seal haulouts occur at Point Francis, on the south end of Portage Island and on Point Migley on Lummi Island's north end. Seals are common in the pass. Gray whales also have been seen in the passage. The nearby wetlands of the Nooksack River delta offer an outstanding winter birding opportunity. Tundra and trumpeter swans are among its visitors.

PORT ANGELES/ VICTORIA

The Port-Angeles-to-Victoria ferry ride gives the ferryboat naturalist an experience in scale—the Strait of Juan de Fuca itself, broad and rolling with robust ocean swells; landforms pale and distant; a western horizon that rolls away for thousands of miles; weather conditions that reduce visibility to zero. For practical purposes, you may as well be on the open ocean. The *Coho* itself reminds you of the difference. It doesn't have the city-bus flavor of a double-ended inland Puget Sound ferry; its lines are seagoing lines—an honest-to-goodness ship with a pointed bow and blunt stern.

This route differs from others on Puget Sound because it crosses a boundary between two very different geological worlds. It leaves a young landscape of lowland glacial deposits and enters an older one where the scouring action of glaciers revealed rocks hundreds of millions of years old. It bridges a seam in the earth's crust. On the south are the young (15 to 35 million years) Olympic Mountains. On the north are the old fragments of a "super terrane" known as Wrangellia, which formed more than 100 million years ago and wandered over the Pacific Ocean crust on a tectonic walkabout before being smeared along the edge of North America from Idaho to Alaska.

Crossing the Strait is also a brush with myth and history. Well into the 18th century, persistent rumors of a "Northwest Passage" fueled the empire-building ambitions of the great European powers. Control over trade routes and commercial monopolies formed the basis of world dominance. England, Spain and Russia were all players in this global game, and the Northwest Coast was, for a time, one of the most important playing fields. The Spanish, alarmed at the Russian presence in what is now Alaska, moved quickly from bases in Mexico to explore and claim as much of the Pacific coast as possible. Although the circumstances of the supposed voyage of "Juan de Fuca" are highly suspicious, enough of a rumor emerged of the Strait of Anian, connecting the Atlantic to the Pacific at about Latitude 48 N, that reputable sailors noted the region with special interest.

The Strait got its name from a Greek ship's pilot in the employ of the Spanish. Apostolos Valerianos (aka Juan de Fuca) claimed to have discovered the cleft in the continent in the late 16th century. His story had its believers as well as its detractors. Although somewhat preposterous even for its day, Juan de Fuca's tale brought several generations of mariners to the region. Captain James Cook, the European discoverer of Australia, New Zealand and Hawaii, approached the intersection of N. Lat. 48 and the Pacific coast in 1789, saw nothing, and was blown back out to sea without venturing farther. Cape Flattery, at the Strait's entrance, was named by him ("it flattered us with the hope of finding a harbour"). Spaniards Estevan Jose Martínez, Francisco de Eliza and Manuel Quimper knew more or less of a deep inlet in the coast from their various journeys from Mexico to their northern base of operations at Nootka Sound. Nevertheless, they made little of the discovery—theirs were not missions to bridge North Pacific to North Atlantic, but to guard Spain's northern flank in the Pacific from the Russians and English.

In 1792, Vancouver entered the Strait, charted its southern shore and entered its southern extension, Admiralty Inlet (generally known today as Puget Sound). Although the geographical reality of the Strait disappointed some because it was no Northwest Passage, Puget Sound itself was a fair consolation. After the Spaniards retreated from the

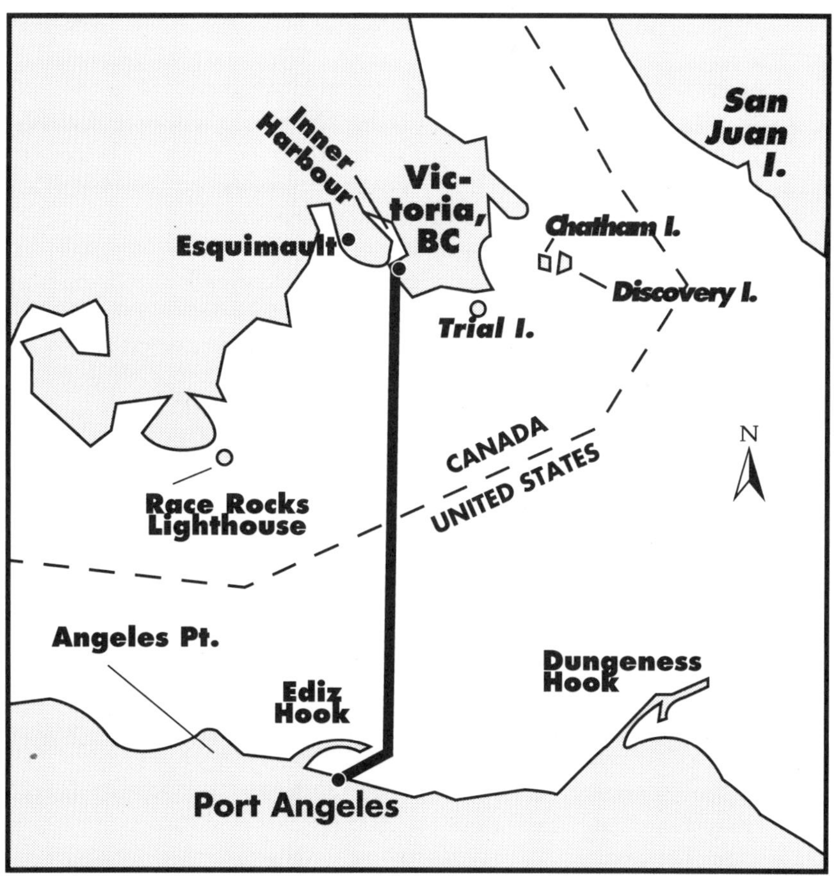

Northwest Coast, Great Britain and the emerging United States continued to claim the territory that is now the Puget Sound region. Only in 1846, with the Treaty of Oregon, did Great Britain concede the Strait of Juan de Fuca as the international boundary.

Port Angeles Harbor

Port Angeles hunkers beneath the imposing bulk of Mt. Angeles (5,464 ft.). Mt. Angeles is composed primarily of tilted layers of volcanic debris and sedimentary rock that formed on the ocean floor between 15 and 30 million years ago. Since then, the slow conveyor belt of tectonic movement has brought the ocean-floor deposits and the North American continent together. With the collision, the Olympic Mountains were formed—a large rumple in the earth's crustal carpet.

During the last Ice Age, at least three large glaciers clung to the north face of Mt. Angeles, forming the cirque basins visible in the upper drainages. The lowlands in the foreground (including the city of Port Angeles) are composed mostly of glacial debris from the Vashon glacial advance about 15,000 years ago, and gravel carried out of the Olympic Mountains by the mountain's glaciers. The waterfront has undergone dramatic changes since the town's founding. Initially it consisted of a row of buildings set upon spindly piers that ran out over the cobble beach. Today, the shore is walled and covered. The downtown area sits on fill sluiced out of the bluffs.

Practically next door to the ferry terminal is City Pier, with its observation tower and the Arthur D. Feiro Marine Lab. The marine lab is a marine environmental education center open to the public. Aquaria and other exhibits display fishes and marine invertebrates of the Strait. Summer ferry travelers who find themselves waiting out long delays between ferries should not delay in finding the marine lab. Hours spent there easily mitigate the discomfort of waiting.

The Port Angeles harbor is one of nature's finest. The long sweeping arm of Ediz Hook shelters the harbor from wave conditions created by ocean swells and strong westerly breezes. A hard mud bottom holds anchors well and the entire harbor is free of shoals. Ediz Hook itself is a textbook example of spit deposition. Like its larger sibling to the east, Dungeness Spit, Ediz Hook has been created by strong wave action from the west, which pounds relentlessly against the soft bluff deposits of the lowland shores. Ediz Hook once benefited from the great sediment burden of the Elwha River, which empties into the Strait five miles west of Port Angeles. Early in this century, two dams were constructed on the Elwha, obstructing the flow of sand and gravel from the eroding Olympic Mountains. Since then, Ediz Hook has been starved of sediments and suffered severe erosion. Presently, the only thing preventing Ediz Hook from eroding away is the massive (and very expensive) armor of rip-rap placed on its northern shoreline.

As the ferry slips away from the dock, look for gulls, cormorants, grebes, loons and other harbor birds. Throughout the year, thousands of gulls congregate here, often sitting on logs stored in large rafts along the southern shore of the Hook. With the benefit of fish-processing plants along the waterfront and the comings and goings of fishing boats, gulls have plenty to feed on.

Port Angeles harbor hosts many harbor seals and river otters. During the summer months, California sea lions often are seen along the waterfront. Occasionally during the winter, California gray whales venture into the harbor. These animals most often are immature males that winter in northern coastal waters rather than complete the trip to Baja California bays where the grays birth their calves.

The sandy bottom of the nearshore area is outstanding habitat for Dungeness and rock crabs. A few patches of eelgrass grow along the edge of the water.

During the first few minutes of the ferry ride, the ship crosses the harbor toward the tip of Ediz Hook. The end of the hook is occupied by a Coast Guard post supporting helicopter and other operations. Familiarize yourself with the positions of the two major pulp mills on the waterfront. One marks the eastern end of the Port Angeles waterfront; the other the western end. Their steam plumes will help you orient your position from the distance as you look back at the Olympic Mountains.

As the ferry passes the tip of the spit, notice the steepness of the beach. The dropoff here is sudden, falling to about 120 feet very quickly. The area off the tip of the spit is well known to salmon anglers, who gather during summer months for chinook salmon. Chinook migrate deep along the kelp beds, pursuing herring and other forage fish that seek the kelp's shelter.

As the distance between ferry and Port Angeles grows, the view of the Olympics changes intriguingly. The dominating hulk of Mt. Angeles takes its place as only one of several imposing summits that front the Strait of Juan de Fuca. Visible east of Mt. Angeles are Blue Mountain and the peaks of the range's northeast corner, Mt. Tyler and Mt. Baldy. West of Port Angeles, the deep cleft of the Elwha River breaks the skyline with its deep blue valley. A welter of peaks lines the horizon to the west, some appearing to emerge right at water's edge.

The Strait of Juan de Fuca is a meteorological "melting pot." Its wave climate is influenced strongly by ocean swells and wind conditions that are, in turn, influenced by a complex set of factors. Highly variable regional weather conditions, and the topography of the

Olympic Mountains, Vancouver Island, the Puget Trough and the Cascade Mountains can create very unusual wind patterns. One condition is known as "the Ediz Hook Eddy." Under certain circumstances, a large counterclockwise rotation occurs in the eastern strait. Winds on the Canadian side blow to the south or west, winds near Port Angeles blow east, and winds at Smith Island blow north. This effect occurs when winds in the strait generally originate in the east—caused by high-pressure air sitting over the land with low-pressure air offshore. Air moving north through the Puget Trough meets air moving south through the San Juan Islands and over the southern tip of Vancouver Island, and other air pours westward out of the Cascades through the Skagit and other river valleys. With such locally variable wind conditions, seas can be unpredictable. Boats under sail can meet wildly variable wind conditions within a relatively small area.

Summer crossings often occur in fog despite warm and clear weather conditions on land. The Port Angeles-Victoria crossing is notorious for casting strong doubts about the remainder of a visitor's vacation. Fear not. If you leave Port Angeles under spectacular weather conditions and encounter pea-soup fog in the Strait, weather in Victoria will be perfect. Summer fog in the strait is known as "sea fog."

A high-pressure system off our coast blows warm, wet air inland. Frequently, that air is cooled right at sea level by the cold water, creating fog. Sea fog is rarely more than 500 feet thick. Over land, where the ground warms the air, the mist evaporates and the fog clears.

During the late summer, fall and winter months another type of fog occurs. This is known as "radiation fog." Radiation fog is formed when no clouds are present to trap the heat of the earth, hence it "radiates" into space during the night, leaving the ground cold. Moisture droplets condense into mist as they contact the cold ground. Sunlight gradually disperses radiation fog—shortly after sunrise when the nights are relatively short, and progressively later as hours of darkness increase with winter's approach. Radiation fog played a large part in obscuring the Port Angeles harbor in 1985, when the *ARCO Anchorage* spilled 249,000 gallons of Alaska crude oil in the harbor. Nearly a week passed before fog conditions slackened, making aerial surveys of the spreading oil difficult.

On clear days, the Race Rocks Lighthouse is visible to the northwest. This light was commissioned in 1861; stone for its construction was quarried in England and carried by ship around Cape Horn. The lighthouse tower is 105 feet high and has alternating black and white stripes. It sits on Great Race, the largest of a cluster of several small rocks and islets. Race Rocks are important haulout sites for harbor seals, northern sea lions and California sea lions, as well as important breeding grounds for colonies of pelagic cormorants and glaucous-winged gulls. Sea otters seen near Race Rocks probably are visitors from farther north along Vancouver Island.

Vancouver Island

As you approach Vancouver Island, notice the island's terrain. Forest-covered knobs dominate a skyline that gradually rises in elevation to the northwest. The southeastern tip—the Saanich Peninsula—is nearly separated from the rest of the island by waterways carved when the last Fraser-glaciation glaciers poured over the landscape. Over much of its length, Vancouver Island was unable to block the Cordilleran glaciers. Thus the island was scoured as the glacier surmounted the ridge of mountains along the general axis of the island. The highly irregular shoreline of Vancouver Island's west coast results from the drowning of large glacier-carved valleys. As a result, complex, island-studded gulfs and long, winding fjords characterize this shore.

The knobby appearance of the topography around the city of Victoria is the result of glacial erosion of hard rock. Bosses, hillocks and humps are the remnants of erosion-resistant bedrock. The gently rolling terrain of gravel-covered lowland occurs only in the depressions—pockets where gravel filled the low spots.

As the landforms of Victoria's Saanich Peninsula begin to show their detail, notice that the ship has entered a broad embayment extending from Race Rocks on the west to Discovery Island in the northeast. Victoria occupies the shore in the northeastern part of this great arc. Here, the Strait of Juan de Fuca is its widest. The western shore of this broad bight, or bend, follows a SW-NE axis through the Metchosin area. The geology of Metchosin differs dramatically from what lies ahead. To geologists, it is a sliver of Washington State parked in Canada. Like the Olympic Peninsula, which consists mostly of sea floor elevated by collision with the continent, this rugged landscape is ancient sea-floor. These rocks end very dramatically in what is called the Leech River Fault, a contact line extending roughly from the inner corner of the broad embayment at Esquimault northwesterly for about 40 miles, and southeasterly beneath the Strait almost to Port Townsend. Along this fault, the oceanic volcanic crust meets a thin band of rocks related to the Cascade Mountains, known as the Leech River Formation (remains of yet another microcontinent that collided with North America about 55 to 60 million years ago). Only a few miles wide, the Leech River Formation consists of intensely squeezed and reheated sedimentary rocks. The Leech River Formation is bounded by rocks of the Wrangellia "superterrane," which form most of the Saanich Peninsula and underlie the city of Victoria.

Wrangellia dates back nearly to the last major breakup of continents, about 200 million years ago. Scattered island arcs moving as pieces of ocean crust in the ancient Pacific Ocean traveled toward what is now North America for about 100 million years. Beginning about 100 million years ago, Wrangellia collided with North America and spent the next 50 million years being smeared along its western edge until it was spread from near Hells Canyon, Idaho, to the coastal mountains of Alaska near present-day Wrangell (hence its name). Little is known of Wrangellia beneath Washington State because of the recent growth of the Cascade Mountains and the vast basalt shield of the Columbia plateau. Victoria marks the emergence of Wrangellia rocks—they form the major rock component of Vancouver Island. Farther north, Wrangellia surfaces as the Queen Charlotte Islands and makes several more appearances in the mountain ranges of southeast Alaska. Although incomprehensibly vast in terms of time and space, the odyssey of Wrangellia is a vivid illustration of earth's dynamism and helps explain why Victoria's landscape seems so unlike that of the rest of the Puget Sound region.

The final approach to Victoria often is highlighted by a brief appearance of Dall's porpoises. These spritely cetaceans serve as a welcoming party to ships visiting Victoria. On a ship the size of the *Coho*, a visit by the porpoises can go unnoticed, so pay close attention to the bow and the area several hundred yards off the bow in all directions. These little whales create distinctive "roostertails" of water when they surface; often the first sign of them is a group of splashes in the distance, unexplainable by wave conditions. Orcas often pass close to Victoria as they enter the Strait of Haro from the Strait of Juan de Fuca. Chances of seeing these majestic whales are relatively slim because they, like you, are just passing through.

About one hour and 15 minutes out of Port Angeles, the ship nears the entrance to Victoria's Inner Harbour at Point Ogden. A long breakwater extends away from the shore to protect the narrow passageway from waves generated from the south and southeast. The scale of the breakwater itself is not readily apparent from this distance. Up close, the massive 22-ton stone blocks, each painstakingly placed, reveal a remarkable engineering feat (achieved around World War I reportedly at a cost of a mere $19,000). Experts are puzzled over the origin of the stone. The nearest source of similar material (granite) is near Johnstone Strait, approximately 145 miles northwest.

Clearing Ogden Point, the ship enters Victoria's Inner Harbour, a narrow inlet that winds into Victoria's heart. The Inner Harbour forms habitat for seals, seabirds, great blue herons, kingfishers and other wildlife—within earshot of traffic and hawking vendors working the tourist throngs.

The city of Victoria is culturally unique in the Pacific Northwest because of its visible ties to Mother England. Vancouver, British Columbia, long ago achieved dominance as a commercial and industrial capital of Canada's west coast because it is the western terminus of Canada's transcontinental railroads as well as a superb deepwater port. Victoria's importance in Northwest and Puget Sound history comes from its role as military and administrative hub of England's Pacific Northwest following the loss of Puget Sound to the Americans under the 1846 treaty. After abandoning the lucrative agricultural enterprises established at Ft. Nisqually, the Hudson's Bay Company relocated on the rocky tip of Vancouver Island.

The city is a naturalist's delight in itself. The Victoria Natural History Society's book *The Naturalist's Guide to the Victoria Region*, written by Jim Weston and David Stirling, is a fine introduction to Victoria's "uncultivated" side. When the weather precludes outdoor rambles, spend the day in the Royal British Columbia Provincial Museum. Natural history and anthropology exhibits are outstanding and provide a glimpse of the natural legacy that all Pacific Northwesterners share.

SEATTLE/ VICTORIA

The Seattle-to-Victoria ferry ride adds the crowning touch to a ferry boat naturalist's experience of Puget Sound. Several boats make the run—the express is the *Victoria Clipper*, which makes the one-way trip in two-and-a-half hours. The larger *Vancouver Island Princess* and the *Princess Marguerite* spend almost four hours each way. Of the three, the *Princess Marguerite* has the strongest link with history and imparts the greatest sense of bygone elegance. Four hours aboard this lovely ship marveling at the splendid scenery is, dollar for dollar, the best value and, minute by minute, the most exciting ride of the Sound.

The route carries us northward through the Sound from Elliott Bay to the Strait of Juan de Fuca, crossing the east end of the strait to Victoria, on the southern tip of Vancouver Island. Unlike cross-sound routes at narrow points that offer only limited views of Puget Sound's scale, the Victoria run is a succession of changing views through a wide variety of Sound environments. It is a "big picture" trip, enlivened by rich moments: porpoises sound a hundred yards off the bow, then frolic in the wake; the frosty brow of Mt. Rainier suddenly emerges in alpenglow. On this run, be prepared for anything; you may be the one person in 2,000 to see, understand and appreciate the small events that reveal the complexity and drama of the Puget Sound ecosystem.

Preparation definitely helps on this run. The ferry is very crowded during spring and summer months, so prepare to jockey for the best viewing spots. While fellow passengers shuffle for deck chairs, staterooms or soft chairs inside, make your way to the bow. On even the balmiest days, have a sweater and windbreaker handy—the luxuriant sunlight of the Seattle waterfront only lasts until the ship begins to round Magnolia Bluff. Even on hot days, short sleeves won't be any match for the rush of wind from the briskly moving vessel. Once the ship is underway, the sleeveless crowds of the foredeck will dissipate and you will have plenty of elbow room on the bow rail.

Keep your binoculars and birdbook handy. You will be covering a lot of water, so a chart is useful. Do not try to wrestle with a full-sized nautical chart, however: the wind will win. Bound strip charts show important features and remain manageable in heavy breezes.

Seattle Waterfront

Victoria ferries disembark from Pier 69, about one half mile north of Colman Dock. Pier 69 typifies the Seattle waterfront system of

warehouse-lined piers built on pilings over the water. A concrete seawall forms the water/land interface with forests of pilings supporting the wharves. Piling environments are thick with marine invertebrates and fishes. Dockside anglers catch large pile perch and, occasionally, rockfish. The most-frequently-caught fish are sculpins (usually called "bullheads"). As last-minute passengers board the ship, look for small forage fish near the surface on the dock side of the ship. Small shiner perch and sculpins are the most commonly seen, although schools of salmon smolts often cruise the waterfront shore.

Glaucous-winged, herring and California gulls are common waterfront visitors, along with crows and pigeons. Western, eared and red-necked grebes often are seen close to the docks. Large flocks of

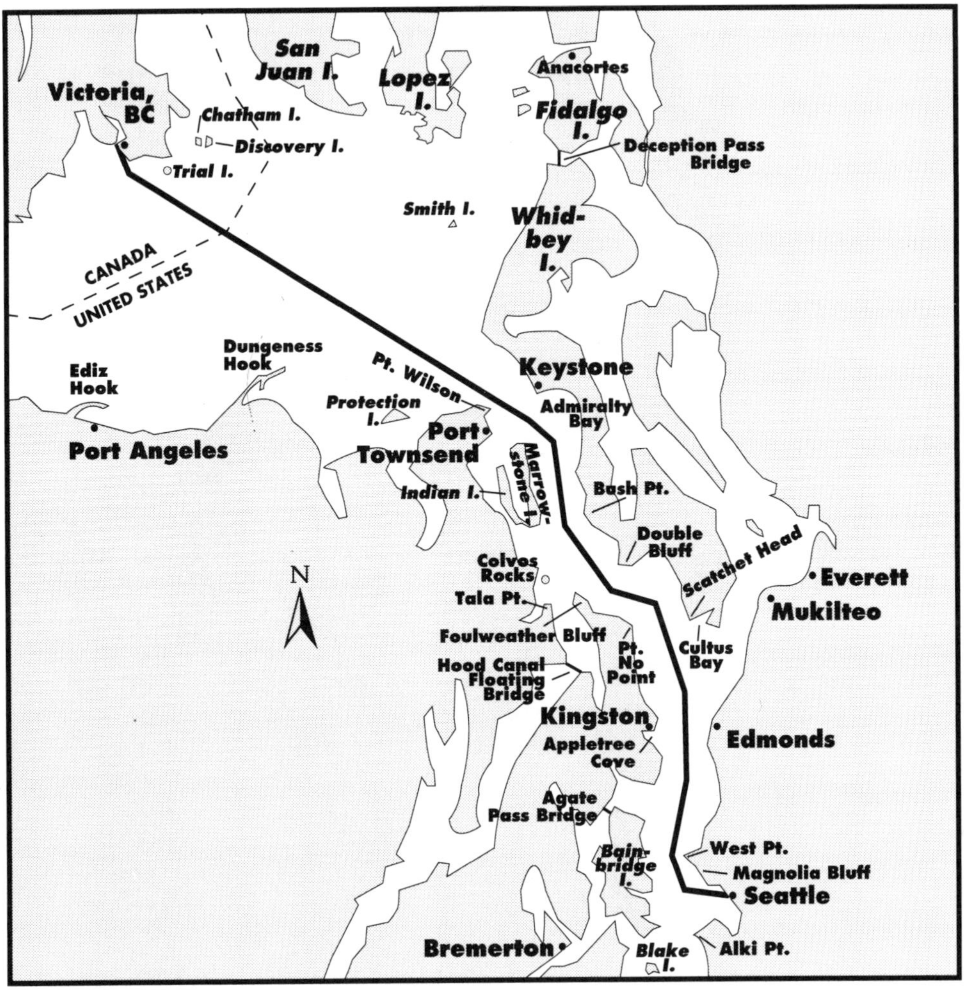

San Juan I.
Lopez I.
Anacortes
Victoria, BC
Chatham I.
Fidalgo I.
Discovery I.
Deception Pass Bridge
Trial I.
Smith I.
Whidbey I.
CANADA
UNITED STATES
Dungeness Hook
Ediz Hook
Pt. Wilson
Keystone
Protection I.
Admiralty Bay
Port Angeles
Port Townsend
Marrowstone I.
Indian I.
Bush Pt.
Double Bluff
Scatchet Head
Colvos Rocks
N
Everett
Tala Pt.
Mukilteo
Foulweather Bluff
Pt. No Point
Cultus Bay
Hood Canal Floating Bridge
Kingston
Appletree Cove
Edmonds
Agate Pass Bridge
West Pt.
Bainbridge I.
Magnolia Bluff
Seattle
Bremerton
Blake I.
Alki Pt.

western grebes frequently appear in spring and summer, cruising and diving together.

Once the lines are cast off and the ship backs from its mooring, the Seattle waterfront becomes visible. To the south, piers extend to East

Waterway of the Duwamish River. Harbor Island, built from fill dredged out of the East and West waterways, sits on what was an extensive tidal flat at the mouth of the Duwamish River. According to some sources, 1,400-acre Harbor Island is the largest man-made island in the world. The Lockheed shipyard flanks the West Waterway of the Duwamish River; the West Seattle Bridge looms overhead. West Seattle is the large land mass southwest of Elliott Bay; Duwamish Head forms the near headland; Alki Beach curves gently toward Alki Point, West Seattle's western tip.

North of Pier 69, commercial wharves lose their grip on the shoreline. Myrtle Edwards Park is in the near foreground, backed by the rounded western slope of Queen Anne Hill. Just beyond the park is the grain terminal. The lowland to the north, known as Interbay, is covered with railyards. Before Seattle grew up around it, the Interbay area was a low marshland at the head of a cleft called Smith Cove.

The bluff that rises west of Interbay is Magnolia Bluff, named for madrona trees explorers mistook for magnolias. Severe landslides scar the bluff face. Gravel and clay comprising the bluffs are glacial legacies and persistent reminders to land-use planners, builders and owners that Puget Sound "view property" is costly for more reasons than scarcity. After it is cleared of vegetation, glacial soil is very susceptible to slope failure, and building on this material requires sound engineering.

West Point, the low point of land at the tip of Magnolia, is formed from sediments eroded out of Magnolia Bluff and carried along the littoral conveyor belt. West Point is distinguished by the large tanks of the West Point Sewage Treatment Plant. Bitter controversy has raged for years over the plant's location on some of Seattle's most scenic shorelands.

Upland of West Point is 535-acre Discovery Park, opened in 1973 following transfer of a large portion of Fort Lawton from the U.S. Army to the City of Seattle. It has become one of Seattle's best-loved natural areas and is restored to its wild condition.

The Sound's central basin is visible to the southwest. Vashon Island occupies the distance; the small, dark form of Blake Island is closer. Puget Sound splits into two channels around Vashon: East Passage lies between Vashon and the eastern mainland; Colvos Passage is to Vashon Island's west. North of Blake Island, Restoration Point marks the southeast corner of Bainbridge Island.

The western horizon is lined with the serrated crests of the Olympic Mountains. The twin summits of The Brothers (6,866 ft.) form the highest peak of the southern skyline; massive Mount Constance (7,743 ft.) towers over its neighbors farther north. A low ridge of hills in the foreground consists of Green Mountain (1,639 ft.) and Gold Mountain (1,761 ft.), located on the central Kitsap Peninsula between Puget Sound and Hood Canal. Astern, majestic Mt. Rainier (14,410 ft.) stands high above the Duwamish waterway.

As the ferry clears West Point, look for Dall's porpoises. A pod of five to seven of the pudgy little black-and-white whales regularly frolics with ships in this vicinity. Their speed is uncanny—sporting with the bow wake of the *Princess Marguerite* means they are traveling as much as 20 knots per hour.

Bainbridge Island

Skiff Point juts eastward from Bainbridge island precisely opposite West Point. The bluffs that line Bainbridge Island reveal more of the pale glacial debris characteristic of the entire Puget Sound region. Using binoculars, you may be able to make out a layered pattern. Such

patterns suggest that the materials were deposited underwater. During the Ice Age in the Puget Sound region, large lakes periodically bordered the vast ice sheet—conspicuous layers of clay, fine sand and silt are the result.

The Bainbridge Island side soon opens into a large inlet known as Port Madison. Points at the south and north ends of Port Madison are named Point Monroe and Point Jefferson, respectively. All three features were named by Lt. Charles Wilkes after the American presidents. Point Monroe is tipped with a long spit that curves around to the west. Nearshore currents along Bainbridge Island run mostly to the north; the spit is formed from sediments eroded off the bluffs mentioned above. Deep within Port Madison is the narrow opening of Agate Passage. This leads into the northern arm of Port Orchard, Bainbridge Island's western moat. Broad beaches, topped by broken bluffs, line the northern shore of Port Madison.

Midway across the entrance to Port Madison, glance southeast for a look at the Seattle skyline towering over Shilshole Bay. Shilshole forms the entrance to the Lake Washington Ship Canal. Shilshole Marina and Golden Gardens Park line the eastern shore. North of Shilshole, the eastern shore is lined with rip-rap to protect the railroad right-of-way. This boulder-covered shore extends northward all the way to Everett.

About 45 minutes out of Pier 69, the ship passes Apple Tree Cove on the west. The town of Kingston nestles on the hill above the water. Kingston is the western end of the Edmonds-to-Kingston ferry run; your ship may slow to let one of the Washington State ferries pass its bow. Edmonds, the eastern end of that ferry route, lies north along the shore. The headland north of Kingston is Apple Cove Point.

North of Edmonds, Puget Sound divides into two channels separated by the blunt end of Whidbey Island. The eastern channel is called Possession Sound and leads to Port Gardner, the Everett harbor. Beyond Everett, the narrow passage extends northward as Saratoga Passage and separates Whidbey Island from the mainland. The western channel is Admiralty Inlet, the main channel of Puget Sound. The south end of Whidbey Island has two conspicuous headlands—Possession Point on the east and Scatchet Head on the west. Cultus Bay separates the two heads. Extensive erosion is visible on the headlands at Whidbey Island's southern tip. Wave energy that travels north through the central basin of Puget Sound collides violently with the soft bluffs. A shallow ledge extends more than two miles southward from Scatchet Head, evidence of the former extent of Whidbey Island. This bank is one of Puget Sound's most popular salmon and bottomfish sport fisheries, itself an indicator of great biological activity. Sport fishermen, gulls and diving birds are abundant.

Cultus Bay gets its name from the Chinook Jargon word for "worthless." Indeed, the bay is very shallow. Although not visible from the ferry, two extensive sand spits line the bay shores. Shore currents from Scatchet Head and Possession Point carry sediment into the bay, making it a trap for material eroded from the battered headlands. Northwest of Scatchet Head is Indian Point. Extensive kelp beds line the shore between Indian Point and Scatchet Head.

Ahead of the ship, notice the blank-wall appearance of bluffs overlooking Useless Bay. As with other south-facing bluffs on Whidbey Island, they receive the full force of waves from Puget Sound's central basin, one of the Sound's longest fetches, and are shaped by wave erosion. Longshore currents move eroding sediments into Useless Bay, where they are trapped in Deer Lagoon.

Point No Point

Look west for the small cluster of red-roofed buildings on Point No Point. Just off Point No Point, the ship turns northwest. Point No Point is significant in history as one of the sites of the Indian treaty signings of 1855. Here, northwest Puget Sound Indian tribes negotiated and ceded most of their land to the U.S. government. Tribes reserved fishing rights, rights confirmed in 1974's famous "Boldt Decision." Today, fishing vessels you see harvesting salmon in Puget Sound are as likely to be operated by tribal fishermen as by non-Indians.

The western shore falls away to the northwest once you pass Point No Point. Crowning the end of the shore is Foulweather Bluff, which obscures the entrance to Hood Canal. The backdrop of the Olympic Mountains tapers toward the horizon. When cloud conditions permit, a low ridge of bluish hills marks the northern end of the Olympic skyline. These hills are collectively known as Blyn Mountain (the ridge extends from the head of Sequim Bay to the head of Discovery Bay) and rise to about 2,000 feet above sea level. As the ship approaches Puget Sound's junction with the Strait of Juan de Fuca, notice its changing position in relation to Blyn Mountain—between Point No Point and Victoria you travel in a great arc, with Blyn Mountain at its approximate center. To imagine the great depth of the ice mass that covered Puget Sound during the last glacial advance, consider that the *summit* of Blyn Mountain was submerged under about 1,600 feet of ice.

Closer at hand, opposite Foulweather Bluff, the ship passes Double Bluff, named for its twin promontories separated by a small cusp of beach. Sediments that comprise the bluffs at Double Bluff are among the oldest of the Puget Sound region, dating back as far as 200,000 to 300,000 years. Atop the Double Bluff sediments are materials from the Whidbey Formation, dating to between 100,000 and 150,000 years before the present.

Massive tide rips occur in the water between Double Bluff and Point Wilson, farther to the north. A large quantity of water flows past Foulweather Bluff in and out of Hood Canal. Eddies form in the shallow embayments to both sides of the channel. Strong winds and heavy flood or ebb conditions combine to make this reach of the Sound particularly treacherous. Aboard ship, these conditions are not hazardous. In fact, they present a dazzling show of force as great quantities of water interact. The convergence zones created by countering currents are biologically rich environments. Seabirds and marine mammals often work the eddyline or tide rip, feeding on schools of fish or drifting plankton trapped between the currents. Watch carefully as the ship approaches areas where the surface texture of the water changes—these shifting "edge" environments host the greatest diversity of organisms of any open water habitats.

North of Double Bluff, the east side of the Sound dips into Mutiny Bay. In clear weather, Mount Baker (10,778 ft.) stands proudly to the northeast. On the ebb tide, a large eddy forms in Mutiny Bay.

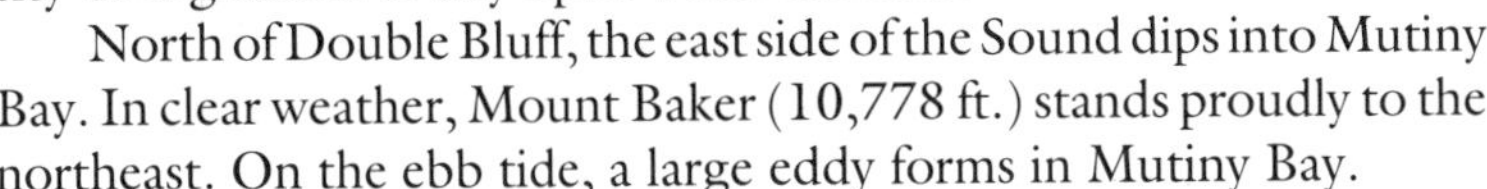

To the west, a large bay opens around the point of Foulweather Bluff. Two bay entrances are actually visible—easternmost is the entrance to Hood Canal. Tala Point sits opposite Foulweather Bluff, guarding the entrance to Port Ludlow. Farther north along the western shore are several rocks, inconspicuous at this distance. Colvos Rocks, Snake Rock and Klas Rock all are part of an exposure of basalt that occurs near the entrance to Mats Mats Bay. (These features are usually difficult to see.) This basalt is part of the oceanic crust that comprises a broad horseshoe partly circling the Olympic Mountains. It is one of the few places south of Admiralty Inlet where old bedrock surfaces along the shores of Puget Sound.

Marrowstone Island and Admiralty Bay

Northwest is Oak Bay, named for small stands of oak trees along its northern shore. Oak Bay is connected to Port Townsend Bay by a narrow, dredged channel at its head. Indian and Marrowstone islands form the northern shore of Oak Bay. The southernmost point of Marrowstone Island is Kinney Point; Liplip Point protrudes a short distance north of Kinney Point.

Buff-colored seacliffs line the shore of Marrowstone Island. Vancouver remarked on the material in his journal: "In most of my excursions I met with an indurated clay, much resembling fuller's earth. The high steep cliff, forming the point of land we're now upon seemed to be principally composed of this matter; which, on a more close examination, appeared to be a rich species of the marrowstone...." Fuller's earth, in Vancouver's day, was a clay that was rubbed into raw wool to absorb the lanolin. When washed, the natural oils would come off with the clay. The shores of Marrowstone consist of layers of clay, sand and gravel from the Vashon glaciation.

Along the eastern shore, look for Bush Point, a low cuspate foreland composed of sediments deposited by longshore currents that converge here. As elsewhere along this reach of the Sound, eddies form in the coves—the bay north of Bush Point whirls in a large clockwise eddy; on the ebbing tide, a heavy rip occurs off the tip of the point itself.

Ahead, Admiralty Bay opens into a broad, curving crescent on the eastern shore. Ship traffic bears closer to the Marrowstone Island side where the channel is deepest. Admiralty Bay forms the largest countercurrent eddy in the northern part of Puget Sound. Both flood and ebb tide currents hug the eastern shore, moving in a counterclockwise pattern, and then collide at right angles with the main current flow at Admiralty Head, just off the ferry harbor at Keystone. Close encounters with this great rip are best experienced on the Port Townsend-Keystone ferry route.

Stay alert for an appearance by a pod of Dall's porpoises in the Admiralty Bay vicinity. They often approach the Victoria ferry and are frequently seen on the cross-sound route as well.

About two hours out of Seattle, the ferry approaches and makes a slight turn at Marrowstone Point. The view into Port Townsend Bay opens to the west. The grassy expanse of Fort Flagler State Park crowns the point. Beyond, the colorful townscape of Port Townsend covers the hillside. Against the backdrop of Blyn Mountain and the northeastern Olympic Mountains, the Port Townsend paper mill billows a landmark steam plume. North of Marrowstone Point, a broad bank extends across the entrance to Port Townsend Bay. This is the Midchannel Bank, and the intensity of biological activity here usually is attested by swarms of gulls, rhinoceros auklets, other birds and a flotilla of sport fishermen. Water depth is about 50 to 80 feet over much of the bank; salmon and bottomfish like halibut and lingcod are attracted to the large underwater plateau to feed on abundant forage fish.

Ahead on the west, Pt. Wilson marks the "corner" of Admiralty Inlet (Puget Sound) and the fabled Strait of Juan de Fuca. Pt. Wilson is located in Fort Worden State Park. The point is a low cuspate foreland covered with dunes and stunted fir trees. Its neat lighthouse began service in 1879 under the hand of David M. Littlefield, a Civil War veteran.

On the east side of the Sound, Admiralty Head guards the tiny harbor at Keystone. Fort Casey sits upon the bluff at Admiralty Head. Together, Forts Casey, Worden and Flagler formed an iron triangle of heavy artillery batteries designed to repel invaders from Puget Sound. Begun half-heartedly in 1896, the three-fort project became a high priority following the sinking of the U.S.S. *Maine* in Havana Harbor

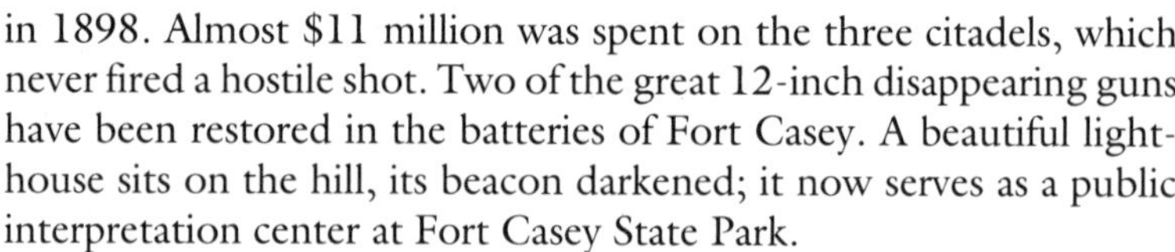

in 1898. Almost $11 million was spent on the three citadels, which never fired a hostile shot. Two of the great 12-inch disappearing guns have been restored in the batteries of Fort Casey. A beautiful lighthouse sits on the hill, its beacon darkened; it now serves as a public interpretation center at Fort Casey State Park.

The Whidbey Island shore is lined with eroded bluffs. Here, the prevailing wave climate is from the west, formed by ocean swells that penetrate the Strait of Juan de Fuca. The graceful lines of the bluffs reflect their "angle of repose," that is, the precise angle at which the soft material can maintain its slope.

As the ferry rounds Pt. Wilson, a new horizon opens to the west. Peeking around the headland along the shore, you will see Protection Island with its pale bluffs and distinctive flagged trees. Protection was named by Vancouver for its strategic placement at the mouth of Discovery Bay. The island previously had been named Isla de Carrasco by the Spanish. Carrasco's Isle originally honored Spanish ships' pilot Juan Carrasco, who discovered it.

Admiralty Sill

The next few minutes are spent over one of Puget Sound's most important bottom features—the Admiralty Sill. The significance of this feature is not immediately apparent. It is, however, both the link that connects Puget Sound to the world ocean and the shallow threshold that gives Puget Sound its unique identity as a marine environment.

Sills form the boundaries of marine basins. Each of Puget Sound's major basins—the Southern, the Central, the Whidbey and the Hood Canal basins—possesses a chemistry of its own, due to the mix of freshwater and silt from rivers, the physical configuration of the basin, its flushing characteristics, the amount of turbulence and water temperature. Sills limit the movement of water between basins to the upper layers—deeper water remains trapped in the basin and only a small part of it mixes with the water exchanged on a given flood or ebb. Thus, the Admiralty Sill acts as the lip of a large containment vessel (Puget Sound), which itself consists of several smaller vessels.

Residence time varies in the basins. A given water parcel may enter the Sound as freshwater from, say, the Nisqually River, and spend several weeks in the Southern Basin before mixing occurs at the Tacoma Narrows and part of the water enters the Central Basin. Several months may be required for it to move through the Central Basin and partially pass over the Admiralty Sill into the Strait of Juan de Fuca to mix with water characteristic of the Pacific Ocean.

Mixing that occurs at the sills is very important biologically. Turbulence caused by water movement through an area of constriction allows nutrient-rich bottom sediments to be brought to the surface where sunlight, the driver of photosynthesis, is abundant. Although turbulence itself suppresses intense biological activity, areas where the well blended "upper" and "lower" waters calm down are very productive. Sunlight penetrating well mixed water helps produce large blooms of phytoplankton "downstream" (generally seaward of the mixing area), in turn giving rise to the whole food chain of plankton feeders and their predators.

It should come as no surprise, therefore, that waters adjacent to Admiralty Sill are very productive. The turbulence visible as large rips in the general vicinity (particularly near headlands and in bays) gives a clue to the intensity of seawater mixing that occurs here. Sport fishermen, and marine birds and mammals in turn, reveal the biological consequence of this great tidal blender.

The eastern Strait

After crossing the sill, the ferry makes its course for Victoria about 30 miles distant, across the broad inland sea of the eastern Strait. Shores recede in every direction; whole islands are but smudges on the horizon. The crossing is anything but featureless, however, for the ship passes that part of Puget Sound that bears the closest resemblance to the open ocean. Waves are formed from winds that can descend from nearly any direction; broad swells roll in from the Pacific; migrant birds like shearwaters and storm petrels—rare inland—work the surface; and knots of kelp, driftwood and eelgrass gather into irregular rafts where widely disparate currents converge.

Look south for Protection Island and northeast for Smith Island. Both these small islands are parts of the National Wildlife Refuge system, designated to protect nesting colonies for seabirds and as haulout sites for marine mammals—mainly seals.

During the spring and summer months, notice the abundance of rhinoceros auklets, which nest in large numbers on Protection and Smith islands. Their blunt forms, strong flight and—if you see them close up—distinctive horned bills make them easy to identify. Look too for tufted puffins. Nesting populations occur at both the island refuges.

The San Juan Islands are strung along the northern horizon. From the left, the foreground is occupied by the long, parched, southwestern shore of San Juan Island. Mt. Dallas (1,936 ft.) is the highest point on the island. The blanched prairie ends at Cattle Point, San Juan's southeastern tip. Cattle Pass—also known as Middle, or San Juan Channel—separates San Juan Island from Lopez Island. Lopez Island fronts the strait with its rocky shores barely discernible from this distance. Acting as a backdrop for Lopez and San Juan islands is the

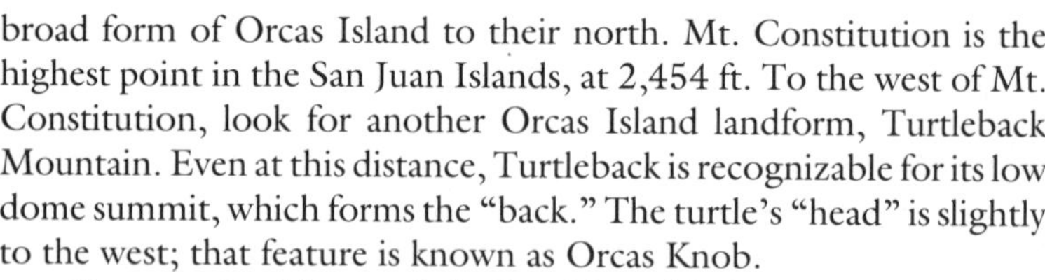

broad form of Orcas Island to their north. Mt. Constitution is the highest point in the San Juan Islands, at 2,454 ft. To the west of Mt. Constitution, look for another Orcas Island landform, Turtleback Mountain. Even at this distance, Turtleback is recognizable for its low dome summit, which forms the "back." The turtle's "head" is slightly to the west; that feature is known as Orcas Knob.

Closer to the ship, watch for Leach's and fork-tailed storm petrels among rafts of floating debris. These birds of the open ocean are rarely seen farther inland. Petrels are distinctive in their twisting and darting flight just above the water. Leach's storm petrels are dark, with a conspicuous white patch on their rump; fork-tailed petrels are gray in color with light bars on their wings. Petrels are sometimes seen "pattering" the water with their spindly feet. They feed on tiny fish, zooplankton and bits of floating debris. Leach's storm petrels are some of Washington's most prolific coastal bird populations—several hundred thousand are known to nest on tiny islets off Washington's outer coast.

Other birds to watch for include sooty shearwaters, long-winged seabirds that soar just above the wave-tops. Common murres, marbled murrelets and pigeon guillamots will be feeding on fish. Pelagic and double-crested cormorants perch on logs and other floating debris that drift about this broad reach of water. Black brant occasionally gather in small groups in these offshore waters. Brant are small black geese easily distinguished by a thin white collar around the neck. During the fall and spring months, large flocks of brant gather along the Olympic shore to feed on eelgrass in the Dungeness Bay estuary and along the beach at Jamestown.

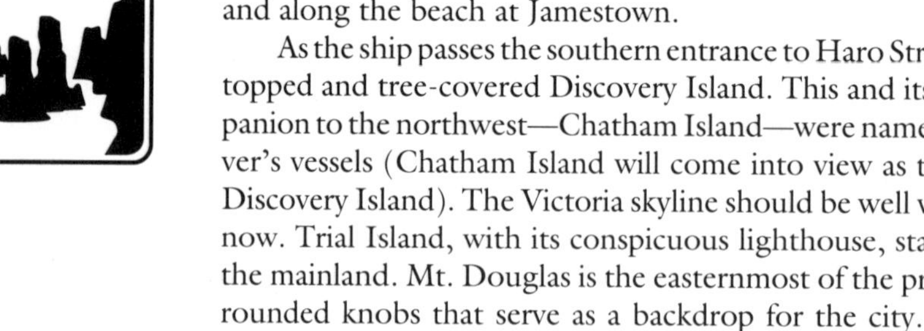

As the ship passes the southern entrance to Haro Strait, notice flat-topped and tree-covered Discovery Island. This and its smaller companion to the northwest—Chatham Island—were named for Vancouver's vessels (Chatham Island will come into view as the ship passes Discovery Island). The Victoria skyline should be well within sight by now. Trial Island, with its conspicuous lighthouse, stands closest to the mainland. Mt. Douglas is the easternmost of the prominent, well rounded knobs that serve as a backdrop for the city. This shape is characteristic of glacial landscapes, where bedrock at the surface was eroded by the advancing ice. As you will see when you enter Inner Harbor, Victoria sits on hard rock—very different from the geologic environment of the Puget lowlands south of the San Juans.

Past Trial Island, three points of land are visible along the Victoria shore: Harling, Clover and Ogden points. All three are outstanding birding sites for the landbound, and well worth visiting. A wide variety of shorebirds, dabbling ducks and seabirds can be seen, including oldsquaws, Harlequin ducks, scoters and peregrine falcons.

This shoreline bears the brunt of the wave climate generated by southeasterly winds in the eastern Strait of Juan de Fuca. Wave erosion has carved an extensive wave terrace, which is exposed at very low tides. Marine life is diverse and abundant. In several locations, glacial erratics—boulders dropped by the glacier, which have very different origins than the surrounding rocks—are perched along the shore.

As the ship approaches land, look out for a pod of Dall's porpoises, playful little whales that frequently approach vessels near the entrance to Victoria's harbor. Other marine mammals commonly sighted near the southern tip of Vancouver Island include orcas, California and Northern sea lions, gray whales, Minke whales and harbor porpoises.

Victoria shore

As the ship skirts the southern shore of Victoria, notice the wooded area above water's edge, about midway along the shore. Beacon Hill Park, Victoria's largest, consists of patchy oak woodlands, scattered natural meadows and manicured parkland. It is an outstanding place to visit year-round, because of its diverse birdlife; during the spring, the park is abloom with both cultivated and wild gardens. Many of the open meadows are left unmowed and host broad expanses of blue-flowered camas, the starch staple of Indians that thrives in sunny meadows with loose soil.

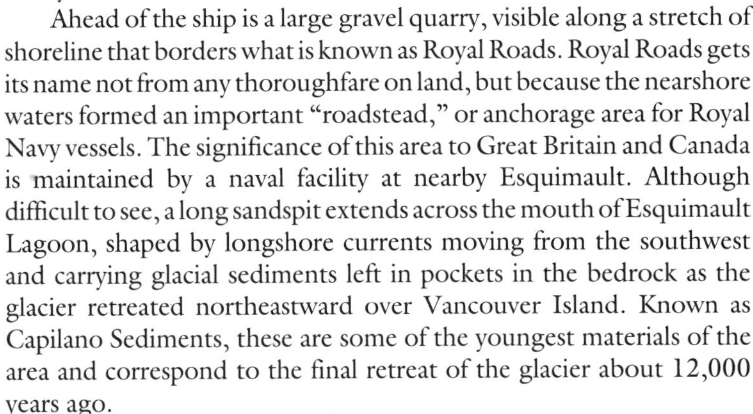

Ahead of the ship is a large gravel quarry, visible along a stretch of shoreline that borders what is known as Royal Roads. Royal Roads gets its name not from any thoroughfare on land, but because the nearshore waters formed an important "roadstead," or anchorage area for Royal Navy vessels. The significance of this area to Great Britain and Canada is maintained by a naval facility at nearby Esquimault. Although difficult to see, a long sandspit extends across the mouth of Esquimault Lagoon, shaped by longshore currents moving from the southwest and carrying glacial sediments left in pockets in the bedrock as the glacier retreated northeastward over Vancouver Island. Known as Capilano Sediments, these are some of the youngest materials of the area and correspond to the final retreat of the glacier about 12,000 years ago.

At Ogden Point, the ship passes into Victoria's Inner Harbour. The Ogden Point breakwater is constructed of giant blocks, neatly placed together. Victoria birders visit Ogden Point breakwater during foul weather to glimpse pelagic birds that are driven closer to shore by inclement conditions.

Entering the harbor, the *Princess Marguerite* and *Victoria Clipper* travel deep into the narrow, rock-lined channel. The *Vancouver Island Princess* stays outside because of its deeper draft and larger size, tying up at the cruise-ship terminal just inside Ogden Point. The *Princess*

Marguerite docks along the south shore of the narrow waterway; the *Victoria Clipper* in the northeast corner.

Victoria's Inner Harbour is a deep cleft in bedrock of very distant origin—both in time and place. The principal rock of downtown Victoria is known as Wark gneiss. This rock probably exceeds 200 million years in age, and is thought to have been formed as oceanic volcanic rock somewhere south of the present equator. About 160 million years ago, Wark gneiss was reheated and partially remelted by other volcanic rock forced into it. The younger rocks are known as the Island Intrusions; outcrops of both ancient bedrock types are found throughout Victoria and along the southern shore of the Saanich Peninsula. An outstanding place to view Victoria's glacier-etched bedrock is at Confederation Fountain, located about one block west of the Parliament buildings.

No naturalist's tour of Victoria would be complete without a visit

to the Royal British Columbia Provincial Museum. British Columbia natural history and cultural history are masterfully presented here. On quick visits to Victoria, or when inclement weather precludes extended outdoor jaunts, a day spent in the museum can equal one spent afield.

The return ferry ride to Seattle will present different light conditions. In the afternoon or evening, bluffs along the eastern shore of the Sound will be displayed in greater detail. Late in the day, the western shore is obscured in the shade. Likewise, notice differences in tide, current and wind conditions. Areas where seabirds were absent on the earlier passage may teem with them if winds and seas have calmed or currents have changed. Noticing these variables will reinforce your understanding that the Puget Sound environment always is changing—seasons, tides, weather patterns, light conditions and fluid wildlife populations promise a new experience with each outing.

SAN JUAN ISLANDS

The San Juan Islands are among Washington's most spectacular landscapes. The archipelago encompasses almost 900 square miles and consists of more than 780 islands and rocks that appear above water at the lowest tides. Here, marine and terrestrial communities of plants and animals are scattered profusely. Dark forests and plowed fields border rocky reefs and sand-filled lagoons. Twisted madrona trees line the rocky shores; shy Calypso orchids grace the shaded floor of the forest. With the shift of seasons, the ebb and flow of migratory wildlife surges through the islands. Visitors consist of wandering seabirds, salmon, whales and waterfowl, each homing to a different call, but converging here because of the islands' vast store of ecological resources.

Fortunately, the ferryboat naturalist has access to the diverse environments and wild inhabitants of the San Juans. With an eye open for marine mammals, birds, geology, shore morphology and the varied texture of plant communities, you will get a good sample of the San Juans. As the ferry moves through the maze-like network of waterways among the islands, scenery and wildlife viewing opportunities arise frequently. Under these circumstances, it's a good idea to start off prepared and stay alert. Several fine books *(Birding in the San Juan Islands*, The Mountaineers; *Wild Plants of the San Juan Islands*, The Mountaineers; and *A Guide to Marine Mammals of Greater Puget Sound*, Islands Press) have been written by experienced local naturalists and can help you prepare even before you step aboard a ferry. Once underway, keep your binoculars, camera, notebook and birdbook handy.

This environment differs dramatically from those elsewhere in the Puget Sound region. Perhaps the greatest difference is the presence of so much hard rock. Landforms of the San Juans consist of high, rounded rocks alternating with gently rolling valleys and plains. In many ways the San Juans can be seen as a deeply eroded mountain range bridging Vancouver Island and the Cascade foothills on the mainland. Some of the rocks of the San Juans are the oldest in the Puget Sound region, formed about 360 million years ago. These rocks are closely related to both the solid bedrock beneath Victoria, B.C. and the crystalline core of parts of the North Cascades. The bedrock geology of the San Juans is a complex subject—tackling it with any detail would require elaboration outside the scope of this book. For the ferryboat naturalist, however, brief references to formations visible from the ferry are included in the trip narrative.

The solid rock of the San Juans was overrun by the Pleistocene glaciers about 15,000 years ago and rounded into knobs. Elsewhere, glacial debris filled the lowlands and hollows, and forms a great part of the landscape of San Juan, Lopez and several other islands.

With the rise of sea level following the retreat of the glaciers, saltwater entered the region. Historically, the network of narrow channels between the Strait of Georgia and its many tributaries to the north, and the Strait of Juan de Fuca and Puget Sound to the south, was called Washington Sound. Surging currents have scoured many of the passages among the islands, making little erosive headway against the bedrock. Where soft glacial debris is licked by waves and currents, erosion has progressed rapidly. Sandy beaches and spits occur mostly on the quiet inner waterways of the island system, where there are sources of glacial debris and waterways of some fetch.

Another important difference is the climate. The San Juans occupy the "rainshadow" of the Olympic Mountains and Vancouver Island. Moist maritime air is forced over higher elevations of the Insular Range of Vancouver Island and the Olympics and sheds much of its water in the mountains as rain and snow. The drier air passes eastward and into the San Juans, resulting in a climate very similar to coastal regions of California. Annual rainfall on San Juan Island's

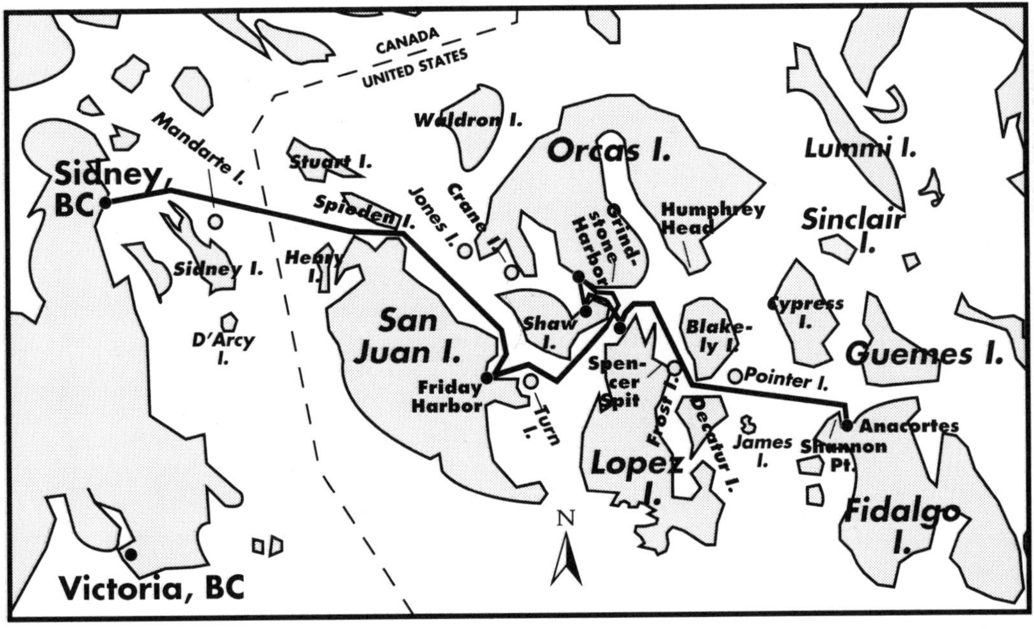

western shore can be as little as 20 inches. The moderating influence of a maritime setting also shapes island climate.

The Washington State Ferry System operates several vessels on this run, and sailings vary in length along a common route. For the sake of clarity, we will begin at Anacortes and end at Sidney, B.C. What you see en route to Lopez, Shaw, Orcas or San Juan Island will be the same as if you were traveling all the way to Sidney.

One variation in the route occurs under certain current and schedule conditions: ferry captains occasionally elect to travel from Orcas Island to San Juan Island by way of Wasp Passage rather than backtrack through Upright Channel between Lopez and Shaw islands. Wasp Passage will be detailed in the following narrative as an alternate route.

This route is frequently overcrowded during the summer months—if you can do without a car on the islands (under most circumstances you won't need one), leave it at Anacortes in the park-and-ride lot downtown. Free shuttle buses make the trip to the ferry terminal.

Anacortes

The Anacortes ferry terminal is actually about three miles west of the city of Anacortes, tucked just east of Shannon Point. To the east, Guemes Channel runs between Fidalgo Island on the south and flat Guemes Island to the north. The Anacortes ferry terminal is located in a slight bay known as Ship Harbor. This bay was once the site of several large canneries, whose wharves extended out to serve deepwater vessels. Just east of the ferry terminal is a small wetland. This salt marsh is a good distraction if you are stuck in traffic waiting for the ferry. Look for kingfishers, crows, great blue herons and other birds of the tidewater/land interface.

On clear days, Mount Baker is visible above Guemes Channel. The southeastern tip of Guemes Island is the only part of the island with any substantial relief; here pre-glacial bedrock forms an outcrop that pierces the mantle of glacial debris. Guemes Channel forms the main shipping channel between Rosario Strait and March Point, the site of several large oil refineries.

North of Shannon Point, Bellingham Channel separates Guemes Island from Cypress Island. The tip of Sinclair Island is visible around Cypress Head, the prominent point along Cypress's eastern shore. Cypress Island dominates the northern foreground. Its stunning relief is a sharp contrast to Guemes Island. The part of Cypress visible from Shannon Point consists of sandstones of the same formation as the Chuckanut Mountains. These rocks are thought to be somewhere just less than 60 million years of age and, in other exposures, contain leaf fossils and poorly formed coal fragments. Cypress Island's highest point is Cypress Dome (1,530 ft.). Cypress Island has no cypress trees;

Captain George Vancouver named it for what we now know as Rocky Mountain junipers, growing as scraggly shrubs along its rocky, sun-warmed slopes (in Vancouver's defense, juniper *is* a member of the cypress family). Reef Point is Cypress Island's southwestern point of land.

The ferry pulls away from the Anacortes terminal and turns west to pass Shannon Point and enter Rosario Strait. West of the strait, the horizon consists of Blakely Island to the north, separated from Decatur Island by Thatcher Pass (the ferry will thread through this narrow opening). In the foreground, the twin humps of James Island sit just in front of Decatur. Behind and south of Decatur is Lopez Island. As the ferry clears Shannon Point and the view opens to the south in Rosario Strait, look southwest for Bird Rocks. This cluster of rocks stands about 30 feet high and hosts breeding populations of glaucous-winged gulls, double-crested cormorants, pelagic cormorants, pigeon guillemots and black oystercatchers. Harbor seals use the rocks as a haulout.

About five minutes out of the ferry terminal, look to the southeast. Burrows Island, with its light, is visible to the south of Fidalgo Head along the eastern edge of Rosario Strait. Shortly, Allan Island becomes visible just beyond Burrows.

Rosario Strait

Rosario Strait is one of the two major passages between the waters of the eastern Strait of Juan de Fuca and the Strait of Georgia. The fact that there are two such waterways led to a serious confrontation between England and the United States following the Oregon Treaty, when Great Britain generally conceded its territorial claims to the Puget Sound region. The agreement was vague as to just which of the channels actually constituted the international boundary. Great Britain considered the Rosario Strait the line, giving it the San Juan Islands. The United States considered Haro Strait, west of the San Juans, to be the boundary, thus making the San Juans American soil. Each country maintained a military presence and at times tension mounted. To learn about the "Pig War," and other details of the joint military occupancy, visit San Juan National Historical Park, on San Juan Island. The matter was settled peaceably through mediation by Kaiser Wilhelm III, who in 1872 heard both sides of the case and ruled that Haro Strait indeed constituted the international boundary. Consequently, with the crossing of Rosario Strait, you are not about to enter Canada.

Near the center of the Strait, look south for a glimpse of Smith Island, with its light. Smith Island is an important breeding site for rhinoceros auklets and tufted puffins. It is part of the National Wildlife Refuge system and therefore protected from development or entry.

Wildlife of Rosario Strait is diverse. Strong currents pour through the four-mile-wide passage and set up covergence zones where they meet the gushes of other passageways and where headlands jut into the tidal thoroughfare. Such zones are very important feeding sites for fishes, birds and marine mammals. During winter months, look for common murres, which gather in large numbers. During summer, phalaropes, terns and several gull species are present in abundance.

Cetaceans known to frequent Rosario Strait include orca and Minke whales, Dall's and harbor porpoises. Harbor seals are common in the strait; several important haulout sites exist here. California and northern sea lions are seasonal visitors.

As the boat nears the gap between Decatur and Blakely islands, a glance far to the north reveals the northern end of Lummi Island in the distance. Tide Point is the spur of land jutting westward from Cypress Island. In the nearer distance, Black Rock, Pointer Island, Armitage Island and Lawson Rock can be seen off the southeast shore of Blakely. Pointer Island is an important glaucous-winged gull nesting site.

The southern view includes twin-humped James Island, separated from Decatur Island by Decatur Bay. Decatur Head is the conspicuous lump connected to the island by a narrow tombolo, a sandspit that actually connects what was once a small island to the mainland shore.

Thatcher Pass

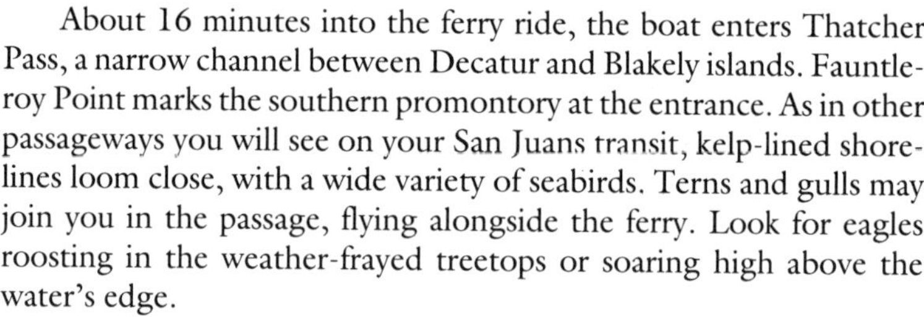

About 16 minutes into the ferry ride, the boat enters Thatcher Pass, a narrow channel between Decatur and Blakely islands. Fauntleroy Point marks the southern promontory at the entrance. As in other passageways you will see on your San Juans transit, kelp-lined shorelines loom close, with a wide variety of seabirds. Terns and gulls may join you in the passage, flying alongside the ferry. Look for eagles roosting in the weather-frayed treetops or soaring high above the water's edge.

About 20 minutes out of Anacortes, the ferry turns northwest, toward Orcas Island. On the southwest, the waters of Lopez Sound separate southern Lopez Island from Decatur Island. Lopez Island lies to the west. Orcas stands high to the north, visible as two ridges, one on either side of the fjord of East Sound. Blakeley Island is to the east. In the near foreground, Frost Island is west of the ferry route. Willow Island stands off the steep slope of Blakeley; the ferry passes closely. Willow Island is a nesting site for pigeon guillemots. White stains on the facing rock are caused by bird droppings.

Lopez Island

West of the ferry lies Lopez Island. Lopez is ranked third in size of the San Juans, with an area of 29 square miles. Topographically,

Lopez is gentler than the other large islands. Most of the island is comprised of rolling terrain, densely forested before white settlement and heavily farmed since then. Most of the island is blanketed by debris of the Vashon glaciation. On its southern coastline, the bedrock foundation of the island is revealed. Pounded by the intense waves of the Strait of Juan de Fuca, the south coastline is pocked with small harbors and flanked with reefs and rocks that defy easy approach from the water. Other major rock outcrops occur, including two ridges that form Humphrey Head and Upright Head at the island's north tip.

Just opposite Willow Island on the Lopez side is Frost Island. To the north is Flower Island. Look for breeding glaucous-winged gulls on Flower and basking harbor seals both on Flower and farther north on Leo Reef, which is marked with a light. Flower is one of many islets among the San Juans that comprise the San Juan Islands National Wildlife Refuge. Entry is forbidden.

From a vantage near Leo Reef, look south along the Lopez shore for a peek at Spencer Spit, a compound sandspit that seems to reach across the narrow pass between Lopez Island and Frost Island. The spit doesn't actually reach the island. Spencer Spit is part of a state park and well worth a visit. A walk along the spit reveals the dynamics of wave, current and shore very vividly. In addition, Spencer Spit is remarkable as habitat for wetland, shore and forest-edge birdlife.

About 32 minutes from Anacortes, the ferry passes Humphrey Head on Lopez Island. In the past, Humphrey Head was a separate island, then gradually was joined to Lopez with the outward growth of an accretionary spit like Spencer Spit. Look for eagles here; a bald eagle nests on Humphrey Head. Shoal Bay, west of Humphrey Head, serves as a collection basin for longshore sediments that converge in the countervailing longshore currents of this intersection of waterways.

West of Shoal Bay is Upright Head, the northernmost point on Lopez and the location of its ferry terminal. Upright primarily is composed of very old sedimentary rocks that tilt to the east. The topography of Upright Head—a steep western face and gentler slope to the east—is due to the bedding of these rocks. About 36 minutes out of Anacortes, the ferry docks at Lopez.

Leaving Lopez, the ferry crosses Upright Channel, which separates Lopez Island from Shaw Island. It rounds Hankin Point, on Shaw Island, then enters Harney Channel, which separates Shaw from Orcas. This narrow waterway averages about one half mile in width. Look along the shores here for eagles and osprey perched in the trees. During fall, winter and spring, large flocks of white-winged scoters gather in the channel.

Look north for several distinctive Orcas Island shore features. Grindstone Harbor, the deepest embayment on Harney Channel, achieved notoriety when a freewheeling ferry captain, on a lark to suit a passenger, guided the ferry *Elwha* onto the rocks at Grindstone's entrance. Needless to say, the incident provoked a lot more than mere embarrassment. Within a few minutes of passing Grindstone, look for a small, unnamed island jutting into the channel from the Orcas side. This knob is attached to Orcas by a thin tombolo, or sandspit.

The ferry hugs the shore of Shaw Island as it travels through Harney Channel. Shaw, at just under 5,000 acres, is the fourth-largest

of the San Juans. It was named by Wilkes for Capt. John D. Shaw, a hero of the War of 1812. Shaw Island is roughly triangular, each of its three sides broken by coves and promontories. The island is generally low, with scattered knobs of rock sticking up through glacial debris. Coniferous forests blanket much of Shaw Island.

At about one hour out of Anacortes, the ferry slips into Shaw Landing. The ferry dock sits on the eastern point of land that guards Blind Bay. Blind Bay is the lower portion of a valley carved by glaciers

as they swept over Shaw. This depression forms a low saddle over the island. On the south side, Indian Cove represents the seawater intrusion into the southern extension of this valley. Situated at the mouth of Blind Bay is Blind Island and a group of rocks known as the Blind Island rocks. Blind Island is a two-acre state park. Its spare skyline is dominated by a large madrona tree.

From Shaw, the ferry makes a quick crossing to Orcas.

Orcas Island

Orcas Island is the largest of the San Juan Islands. Orcas has an area of 58 square miles or about 36,500 acres. Orcas also forms the highest of the islands with its summit on Mt. Constitution at 2,454 feet. Orcas is shaped roughly like a saddlebag, with two major lobes separated by East Sound, a fjord about one mile wide and eight miles long. At its northern end, East Sound terminates in a narrow lowland upon which sits the community of Eastsound. The northern shore of Orcas lies only $1^1/_4$ miles north of the head of East Sound. East Sound, as a narrow slot between highlands on both the landforms that flank it, serves as a wind tunnel in both northerly and southerly winds. Sailors on both sides of the island frequently have to contend with intensely focused gusts channeled through the sound's topographic gauntlet. The lowland connecting Orcas' two lobes is indeed "low." A sea level rise of a mere 20 feet would flood the gap between east and west Orcas and divide the island in two.

The western part of the island also is divided into two lobes. These are separated by West Sound, a harbor about four miles long and one mile wide. The western lobe of Orcas displays considerable relief, although the land does not rise as high as the eastern lobe. Turtleback Mountain forms the high point of the area, with an elevation of 1,500 ft. The name "Turtleback" is an apt description of the landform. This hill is a broad dome composed of very ancient metamorphic rock. The turtle's "head" is another boss of glacier-carved rock known as Orcas Knob, which rises to 1,028 feet on the westernmost lobe of the island. Taken together, Turtleback Mountain and Orcas Knob create a landmark topographical feature than can be seen easily from nearly any vantage point within 50 miles of the San Juans. Comparing the position of the "turtle" with that of Mt. Constitution, you can easily locate the extent of Orcas Island on the horizon.

Wasp Passage Route (the seldom-used shortcut)

Travelers between Orcas and San Juan islands are rarely treated to a remarkable short-cut: passage through the Wasp Islands. Vessel size, tidal stage, time of day and other factors make this a skipper's choice. After the ferry leaves Orcas, it moves westward, across the broad opening of West Sound and around Broken Point on Shaw Island. Broken Point is an excellent example of a once-separated knob of rock that now is connected to a nearby shore by a natural causeway of accreted sand.

The view northward into West Sound is framed beneath the skyline profile of Turtleback Mountain, with Orcas Knob as the turtle's head. Nearer in the foreground, along the western shore of West Sound, is Double Island (the largest of the three small islands) with Alegria Island (locally known as Little Double Island) in the foreground and Victim Island behind. The ferry moves toward wooded Bell Island and passes close to a reef 250 yards east of Bell. Notice rafts of kelp near the reef.

Northwest of Bell, Pole Pass separates Orcas Island from Crane Island. The ferry moves southwest through Wasp Passage, the channel that separates Crane Island from Shaw. Crane Island is about 221 acres in area, with its highest point rising to 120 feet of elevation. In spite of its small size, Crane has a small airstrip and a scattering of residences.

Past Crane Island, Wasp Passage widens. To the northwest, the smaller Wasps make their appearance. Nearest the ferry on the north side is Cliff Island, backed by three small islands strung from southwest to northeast: Yellow, McConnell and Reef. In the foreground between Cliff and these three are several small rockpiles including Low Island (between the ferry and Yellow Island), Nob Island (just off Cliff Island) and Coon Island (between Cliff and McConnell islands). The headland jutting in from the south is Neck Point.

The Wasps form a remarkable ensemble of ecological gems. Terrestrial communities vary from island to island. Several of the islands host mixed coniferous/hardwood forests consisting of Douglas fir, lodgepole pine, Rocky Mountain juniper and Oregon white oak. Several support meadow habitats with startling arrays of wildflowers. Brittle cactus is reported on Yellow and several of the other islets. Of these, Yellow Island is owned by The Nature Conservancy for preservation purposes. Several of the smaller rocks and islands are owned by the U.S. Fish and Wildlife Service and are reserved for wildlife. Because the Wasp group forms such a welter of currents, stay alert for feeding birds and seals among the channels.

Following the exciting transit of the Wasps, the ferry enters San Juan Channel and turns south toward Friday Harbor.

Upright Channel (the normal route)

After the ferry leaves Orcas, it usually returns through Harney Channel to Upright Channel for passage around Shaw Island. Upright Channel runs northeast to southwest, perfectly lined up to serve as a fetch for winds that originate in the southwest. This is the key to understanding the shape of the shoreline on Lopez Island, which sits to the east. Looking ahead as the ferry moves into Upright, you see the foreground occupied by a low point of land on the Lopez side and a winding low-bluff rocky shore on the Shaw side. Canoe Island sits in a bay to the right. Beyond is the broad expanse of Griffin Bay (where the waves form), backed by the low plain of southern San Juan Island. During the summer and fall months, the plains of San Juan are golden, owing to their dryness.

Notice the contrast between the Shaw and Lopez shorelines. Shaw is composed mostly of rocks that resist erosion; Lopez is mostly gravel that has been carved significantly by wave erosion. Flat Point is a prominent depositional feature, a cuspate foreland created by sediments carried along the west shore of Lopez.

During the summer and early autumn months, notice the paired boats, on both sides of Upright Channel but most prominent on the Shaw side. These are reefnet boats, the modern equivalent of canoes used by presettlement Indians in this unique and ancient salmon fishery. The principle used in a reefnet fishery is that salmon navigate among the islands along the shore and the bottom. The reefnet is an artificial bottom (or reef) that fools the fish. They are directed to a narrow portion of the net and into the "bunt," a baglike section of the net. The boats that you see are stationary and anchor the reefnet. Towers on the boats enable observers to watch the progress of the salmon over the reef so that the net can be raised and the fish captured.

After the boat passes the narrows between Flat Point and Canoe Island, look for Turn Island ahead. At the intersection of Upright Channel and San Juan Channel (which runs north and south), the boat turns north for its approach to Friday Harbor.

Before we leave Lopez Island, look along the shore to the southeast of the ferry. The loose cluster of buildings is the village of Lopez, situated above Fisherman Bay. Fisherman Bay is a shallow harbor created by a long enclosing spit. As with Flat Point, wave action originating in the southwest has created a large spit complex. Fisherman Bay is shallow and its entrance is particularly tricky. Nevertheless, it provides generous sanctuary for boaters and is Lopez Island's largest harbor.

San Juan Channel and San Juan Island

San Juan Channel is the north/south "main street" of the islands, forming a direct passage from the Strait of Juan de Fuca to Boundary Pass (which separates the Canadian Gulf Islands from the American San Juans). The ferry will traverse the middle one third of the channel. Before you see much of San Juan Channel, however, the boat makes its stop at Friday Harbor.

After rounding the corner near Turn Island, you see signs of scattered development on San Juan Island. A massive gravel pit in a saddle of the low hills is evidence of a large pocket of glacial material. Although much of San Juan Island is covered with glacial debris, the island is also very rocky.

Look for orcas and Dall's porpoises in San Juan Channel. Although the passage is busy with boat traffic, it is also frequently used by non-human marine travelers, for whom it is equally important as an inter-island thoroughfare.

Friday Harbor

The town of Friday Harbor is tucked in a bay on the island's east side, under the sentinel presence of Brown Island (locally known as Friday Island). The island very effectively protects the harbor from the waterward side; relatively steep hills surrounding the harbor on the landward side also provide shelter.

Two stories account for Friday Harbor's name. According to one, a mariner approached the dock unsure of where he was. Shouting to the shore, he inquired as to the name of the bay. The informant, mistaking the word "bay" for "day," answered "Friday." In the other account, "Friday" is derived from a Hawaiian Hudson's Bay sheepherder whose name was John Friday. Take your pick.

Shortly after entering the narrow passage north of Brown Island, the boat passes the University of Washington Friday Harbor Marine Laboratory. This biological field station, one of the earliest established in the Northwest, is open for visitors.

In addition to the marine lab, ferryboat naturalists will enjoy Friday Harbor's Whale Museum, which provides a wealth of information about the San Juans' most famous wildlife inhabitants.

After leaving Friday, the boat re-enters San Juan Channel, and turns north. Point George, on Shaw Island, is to the east. The ferry passes west of Reid Rock, which rises to about 13 feet below the surface at low tides. Kelp beds and tide rips surround this hidden "fang," which is well marked by a buoy. As the ferry moves northward, it passes Point Caution on the San Juan side.

Wasp Islands

About 15 minutes out of Friday Harbor, the ferry comes alongside the litter of small islands on the right that comprise the Wasp Group. The Wasps form a scattering of small islands partly blocking the channel that separates Orcas Island from Shaw.

The largest of the Wasps is Crane Island, which sits well back from San Juan Channel. In the foreground are Reef, McConnell, Cliff and Yellow islands. Yellow Island is owned by The Nature Conservancy

and is under a strict program of habitat preservation. The driftwood home of its last human inhabitants, Lew and Tib Dodd, is visible on the southwest side of the island, backed by the forest edge. The conservancy purchased the island in 1980 because of the integrity of its native plant communities, which include old-growth forest, meadows and intertidal areas. Wildflowers are particularly stunning here, and access to the island is limited in order to protect the fragile grassland meadows.

Past Yellow Island, the view opens into North Pass, which leads into the Orcas Island port of Deer Harbor. Jones Island lies off Steep Point, the southwestern point of Orcas Island. Reef Island sits between the Wasps and Steep Point.

Jones Island covers 188 acres and is a popular recreational boating destination. The entire island comprises Jones Island Marine State Park. As the ferry cruises this part of San Juan Channel, keep a sharp eye out for eagles and ospreys, which nest at several locations on the San Juan side.

About 20 minutes out of Friday Harbor, when the ferry is opposite Jones Island, look west for O'Neal Island in the broad bight of Rocky Bay. Four-and-one-half-acre O'Neal Island is composed of limestone-bearing rocks similar to those found on Orcas Island and elsewhere on San Juan Island and is reported to have had a quarry. No signs of such activity are obvious, however.

In the distance to the north is Flattop Island. Flattop is distinguished by its profile, which actually shows a slight depression along its skyline. Flattop covers about 50 acres and is composed of sandstone beds that dip slightly to the southeast.

Beyond Flattop is the massive form of Waldron Island, with its dark, sloping beds of shale and sandstone that mark the prow of Point Disney. When the light is right, the bedding of Waldron's sedimentary rocks is easily seen in the 500-foot cliff. On clear days, the peaks of the British Columbia Coast Range form the skyline in the haze-filled distance.

Speiden Channel

About 20 minutes out of Friday Harbor, the ferry turns west from San Juan Channel into Speiden Channel. Limestone Point on San Juan Island marks the southern point at the entrance; Green Point, on Speiden Island, marks the northern point of the entrance. The most distinctive landmark here is the long, sun-baked south-facing shore of Speiden Island. The 480-acre island is a long ridge, crested with a forest that spills over its north slope. The steep south slope, however, is bone-dry and mostly treeless.

Speiden Island has a colorful past in terms of natural history. A previous owner of the island attempted to create a commercial game ranch to lure big-game hunters. The island was stocked with a variety of non-native deer, goats, antelope and wild sheep. The enterprise provoked outrage from sportsmen and environmentalists for its ecological short-sightedness and was short-lived. The consequences remain with us today, however, as some of the animals remain in a wild state and have overgrazed the island.

As Speiden Channel widens, several interesting and biologically important features come into view. Sentinel Island, just off Speiden Island, is about 15 acres in size, and capped with forest cover. Bald eagles nest on the site. The shores also support nesting oystercatchers and pigeon guillemots. Just west of the island is Sentinel Rock, a haulout site for seals and sea lions. Closer to the ferry, look for the buoy and kelp that mark Center Reef.

On the San Juan Island side, the boat passes Davison Head, which stands at the northeast entrance to Roche Harbor. Davison Head is composed of sandstones of the Haro Formation, western Washington's only known formation from the Triassic Period, dating from about 180 to 230 million years ago. Straddling the northern entrance to Roche is 38-acre Pearl Island. Barren Island is the most prominent of the nearer rocks; Posey Island is just north of the west end of Pearl.

Although not visible because of the protection afforded by Pearl Island, Roche Harbor is worth noting for two important reasons. First is its geological significance. This part of San Juan Island is composed of ocean deposits laid down more than 230 million years ago. Within these fine-grained sediments are pockets of limestone. Beginning in 1857, this limestone was quarried, burned in large limekilns and then exported throughout western Washington and as far away as Hawaii and South America. The Roche Harbor Lime and Cement Company operated its quarries until 1956, when supplies were depleted.

Roche Harbor's second distinction is its status as one of the most popular yachting destinations in the San Juans. The elegance of its previous days, when considerable wealth was generated on the site, is maintained in a festive, country-club atmosphere. Boaters enter Roche Harbor through either of the channels around Pearl Island (the western one is deeper) or through its southern entrance, Mosquito Pass.

Just west of Pearl Island is the northern tip of Henry Island, named for Midshipman Wilkes Henry, nephew of Lt. Charles Wilkes, who explored the islands in 1841. Henry had been killed one year earlier while the expedition charted the Fiji Islands. Henry Island covers about one and one half square miles and is formed by two parallel ridges separated by salt water except for a narrow isthmus. The northern tip of Henry Island is McCracken Point.

About one mile west of McCracken Point is Battleship Island. Battleship Island once bore the name Morse Island (named by Wilkes for another of his crewmen) but was changed to Battleship Island because of its ship-like appearance.

Stuart Island

Passing Battleship Island, the ferry enters Haro Strait and moves toward Vancouver Island. Directly north is Stuart Island, the westernmost of the American San Juans. Like many others of the San Juans, Stuart was named by Wilkes, for Frederick D. Stuart, clerk of the ship *Peacock*. The Lummi Indian name was Qunnis, which means "whale." Its high point, Tiptop Hill, is about 650 feet above sea level. Like Speiden, its southern slope is largely clear of vegetation, owing to its sun-warmed aspect. Stuart's shore appears fairly regular from this perspective. In reality the island is convoluted, consisting of folded ridges that run along a northwest-southeast axis. Stuart's rocks are of the Nanaimo series, sandstones between 63 and 100 million years old. Nanaimo rocks form most of the northern San Juan islands, including Stuart, part of Orcas, Sucia, Matia, Patos and Waldron islands. These rocks continue to the northwest and form many of the Gulf Islands. Stuart's northwesternmost point is Turn Point, named because it marks the turning point for vessels bound north in Haro Strait.

Haro Strait

Haro Strait is the broad channel that separates Henry and San Juan islands from the Saanich Peninsula on Vancouver Island and then bends toward the northeast, separating Saturna and Moresby islands on the Canadian side from Stuart and Patos islands in the American San Juans. It also forms the international border between the United States and Canada.

The southern reach of the strait is a 16-mile-long fetch that lies along a north/south axis and funnels winds from either direction. With predominant southerly winds and wave patterns, the movement of longshore sediment is primarily to the north. Only on the Canadian side is this readily apparent—spits, cusps and other depositional features are largely absent on the San Juan Island side because of the hard rock of the island's western shore. Major spit systems occur in the relatively protected waters within Sidney Harbor and are discussed below.

Off Turn Point, the northwesternmost promontory on Stuart Island, the strait bends eastward and continues for about 11 miles, where it connects with the Strait of Georgia.

Haro Strait was named Canal de Haro in 1790 for Gonzalo Lopez de Haro, first mate of Spanish explorer Manuel Quimper. In 1847, the

British naval captain Henry Kellet, who charted much of the Puget Sound region, modified the name to the present "Haro Strait."

Haro Strait presents a mixed bag for naturalists. Generally speaking, it is not as productive as Rosario Strait for seabirds, but it can be extremely exciting for whale sightings. By far, the greatest concentration of orca encounters in the San Juans occurs along the western shore of San Juan Island. Pods frequently are seen near Henry and Stuart islands. Minke whales occasionally are sighted in the massive rips and convergence currents of Haro Strait. Dall's porpoise are very common here. You will usually see them first in the distance, made conspicuous by splashes as they surface.

Although no dotted line marks the international boundary as it runs through the middle of Haro Strait, you can reckon its approximate position. You become an international traveler when the ferry passes a point on an imaginary line extending from the southern tip of Sidney Island to Turn Point, on Stuart Island. Cheers!

Once the ferry has passed the midway mark in Haro Strait, familiarize yourself with the scenery ahead. In the northwest foreground is a cluster of islands consisting of Gooch Island (the nearest), Domville and Brethour islands (northwest of Gooch) and Forrest Island (due west of Gooch). South of the ferry, Mandarte Island is the long, low, barren rock closest at hand; Halibut Island is similarly shaped but located farther south. Sidney Island is the long, forested island forming the backdrop to Mandarte and Halibut. South of Sidney Island are D'Arcy and Little D'Arcy islands. In the extreme distance, seeming to float out of the shimmering water at the southern entrance to Haro Strait, are the thin profiles of Chatham and Discovery islands. On clear days, the skyline of the Olympic Mountains forms a bluish backdrop to the south.

Mandarte and Sidney islands

As the ferry passes Mandarte Island, notice several silvered tree snags. Mandarte is an important nest site for tufted puffins. Double-crested cormorants and glaucous-winged gulls also nest here.

Like Speiden Island, Sidney Island has been planted with several exotic species of mammals; it hosts populations of both the European rabbit and the fallow deer.

Sidney

The final approach to Sidney begins as the ferry rounds Sidney Spit, about one hour out of Friday Harbor. Sidney Spit is a long sandspit that runs northwesterly from the tip of Sidney Island. The spit is formed by the northward movement of sediments eroded out of the northern half of Sidney Island, which is composed of glacial debris.

Once inside, the water calms. This relatively sheltered, shallow water hosts large numbers of seabirds throughout the year. During the winter, however, it teems with birds.

About one hour and 10 minutes from Friday Harbor, the ferry docks at Sidney. Here, you step ashore onto the Saanich Peninsula of Vancouver Island. A trip ashore is necessary, even if you plan to return to Friday Harbor or Anacortes. All round-trip passengers are required to clear Canadian customs before returning to the boat.

If you are headed toward Victoria (17 miles to the south), you are in for a variety of natural-history delights. Birding, spring wildflowers, urban geology, marine biology and museum hopping all await you. Three other ferry routes are within striking distance. The Port Angeles-Victoria (page 130) and Seattle-Victoria (page 138) routes both are fruitful naturalist voyages back to Puget Sound country. Another, the British Columbia ferry route from Swartz Bay to Tsawwassen by way of Active Pass, is extraordinary. For that one, you will have to be your own guide. Bon voyage!

APPENDIX

Marine Education Centers

Pt. Defiance Zoo and Aquarium, Tacoma.
Seattle Aquarium, Seattle.
Pacific Science Center, Seattle.
Poulsbo Marine Science Laboratory, Poulsbo.
Breazeale Interpretive Center, Padilla Bay National Estuarine Sanctuary, Bayview.
Arthur D. Feiro Marine Laboratory, Port Angeles.
Port Townsend Marine Science Center, Port Townsend.
Maritime Heritage Center, Bellingham.
University of Washington Friday Harbor Labs, Friday Harbor.
The Whale Museum, Friday Harbor.

For Further Reading

Weston, Jim, and David Stirling, eds. *The Naturalist's Guide to Victoria*. Victoria, BC: Victoria Natural History Society, 1986.

Alt, David D., and Donald W. Hyndman. *Roadside Geology of Washington*. Missoula, MT: Mountain Press, 1984.

Angell, Tony, and Kenneth C. Balcomb III. *Marine Birds and Mammals of Puget Sound*. Seattle: Puget Sound Books, Washington Sea Grant, University of Washington Press, 1982.

Atkinson, Scott, and Fred Sharpe. *Wild Plants of the San Juan Islands*. Seattle: The Mountaineers, 1985.

Bascom, Willard. *Waves and Beaches*. Doubleday & Co., 1964.

Bell, F. Heward. *The Pacific Halibut: the Resource and the Fishery*. Anchorage: Alaska Northwest Publishing Co., 1981.

Burns, Robert. *The Shape & Form of Puget Sound*. Seattle: Puget Sound Books, Washington Sea Grant, University of Washington Press, 1985.

Chasan, Daniel Jack. *The Water Link: A History of Puget Sound as a Resource*. Seattle: Puget Sound Books, Washington Sea Grant, University of Washington Press, 1981.

Cummings, Al, and Jo Bailey-Cummings. *Gunkholing in the San Juans*. Edmonds: Nor'westing Inc., 1984.

Downing, John. *The Coast of Puget Sound: Its Processes and Development*. Seattle: Puget Sound Books, Washington Sea Grant, University of Washington Press, 1983.

Easterbrook, Don, et al. "Age of the Salmon Springs Glaciation in Washington," *Geology*, Vol. 9 (February 1981), pp. 87-93.

Easterbrook, Don, et al. "Pleistocene Glacial and Interglacial Chronology in Western Washington" (Abstract). Paper presented at Cordilleran Section, Geological Society of America, Anaheim CA, 1982.

Evans-Hamilton, Inc., and D.R. Systems, Inc. *Puget Sound Environmental Atlas.* Seattle: U.S. Environmental Protection Agency, Puget Sound Water Quality Authority and U.S. Army Corps of Engineers, 1987.

Everitt, Robert D., et al. *Marine Mammals of Northern Puget Sound and the Strait of Juan de Fuca, NOAA Technical Memorandum ERL MESA-41.* Boulder: Department of Commerce, NOAA Marine Ecosystems Analysis Program, 1979.

Fischnaller, Steve. *Northwest Shore Dives.* Edmonds: Bio-Marine Images, 1986.

Flora, Charles J., and Eugene Fairbanks, M.D. *The Sound and the Sea.* Bellingham: Western Washington University, 1982.

Gibbs, James A. *Sentinels of the North Pacific.* Portland: Binfords and Mort, 1955.

Gotshall, Daniel W., and Laurence L. Laurent. *Pacific Coast Subtidal Marine Invertebrates.* Monterey: Sea Challengers, 1979.

Harbo, Rick M. *Tidepool and Reef: Marinelife Guide to the Pacific Northwest Coast.* Surrey, BC: Hancock House, 1984.

Ingmanson, Dale E., and William J. Wallace. *Oceanology: an Introduction.* Belmont: Wadsworth Publishing Co., 1973.

Hart, J. L. *Pacific Fishes of Canada.* Ottawa: Fisheries Research Board of Canada, 1973.

Hines, Bob. *Ducks at a Distance: A Waterfowl Identification Guide.* Washington, DC: Department of Interior, U.S. Fish and Wildlife Service. 1978.

Hitchman, Robert. *Place Names of Washington.* Tacoma: Washington State Historical Society, 1985.

Howard, Harry W. *Sport Fishing for Pacific Salmon.* Eugene: Koke-Chapman Co., 1955.

Kline, M.S., and G.A. Bayless. *Ferryboats: A Legend on Puget Sound.* Seattle: Bayless Books, 1983.

Kozloff, Eugene N. *Seashore Life of the Northern Pacific Coast.* Seattle: University of Washington Press, 1983.

Lamb, Andy, and Phil Edgell. *Coastal Fishes of the Pacific Northwest.* Madiera Park, BC: Harbour Publishing Co. Ltd., 1986.

Leatherwood, Stephen, et al. *Whales, Dolphins and Porpoises of the Eastern North Pacific and Adjacent Arctic Waters: A Guide to Their Identification.* New York: Dover Publications, 1988.

Lilly, Kenneth E. *Marine Weather of Western Washington.* Seattle: Starpath School of Navigation, 1983.

Lewis, Mark G., and Fred A. Sharpe. *Birding in the San Juan Islands.* Seattle: The Mountaineers, 1987.

McKee, Bates. *Cascadia: The Geologic Evolution of the Pacific Northwest.* New York: McGraw-Hill Book Co., 1972.

McLellan, Roy D. *The Geology of the San Juan Islands.* Seattle: University of Washington Press, 1927.

Meany, Edmond S. *Origin of Washington Geographic Names.* Seattle: University of Washington Press, 1923.

Mueller, Marge & Ted. *North Puget Sound: Afoot and Afloat.* Seattle: The Mountaineers, 1988.

Mueller, Marge & Ted. *The San Juan Islands: Afoot and Afloat,* 2nd ed.. Seattle: The Mountaineers, 1988.

Mueller, Marge & Ted. *South Puget Sound: Afoot and Afloat.* Seattle: The Mountaineers, 1983.

Osborne, Richard, et al. *A Guide to Marine Mammals of Greater Puget Sound.* Anacortes: Island Publishers, 1988.

Puget Sound Water Quality Authority. *State of the Sound: 1986 Report.* Seattle: Puget Sound Water Quality Authority, 1986.

Robbins, Chandler S., et al. *Birds of North America,* rev. ed. New York: Golden Press, 1983.

Scheffer, Victor B., and John W. Slipp. "Whales and Dolphins of Washington State with a Key to the Cetaceans of the West Coast of North America." *American Midland Naturalist,* Vol. 39, No. 2, March 1948, pp. 257-337.

Scott, James W., and Melly A. Reuling. *Washington Public Shore Guide: Marine Waters.* Seattle: University of Washington Press, 1986.

Strickland, Richard M. *The Fertile Fjord: Plankton in Puget Sound.* Seattle: Puget Sound Books, Washington Sea Grant, University of Washington Press, 1983.

Squire, James L., and Susan E. Smith. *Angler's Guide to the United States Pacific Coast.* Seattle: Department of Commerce, NOAA, National Marine Fisheries Service, 1977.

State of Washington, Department of Ecology. *Coastal Zone Atlas of Washington, Regional Volume IV: Kitsap, Jefferson and Clallam Counties.* Olympia: Department of Ecology, 1979.

Terich, Thomas A. *Living with the Shore of Puget Sound and the Georgia Strait.* Durham: Duke University Press, 1987.

Vancouver, George. *The Voyage of Discovery to the North Pacific Ocean and Round the World 1791-1795,* Vol. II. London: The Hakluyt Society, 1984.

Wahl, Terence R., and Dennis R. Paulson. *A Guide to Bird Finding in Washington.* Bellingham: T. R. Wahl, 1986.

Wahl, Terence R., et al. *Marine Bird Populations of the Strait of Juan de Fuca, Strait of Georgia and Adjacent Waters in 1978 and 1979.* EPA-600/7-81-156. Washington, DC: Environmental Protection Agency, 1981.

Whitebrook, Robert Ballard. *Coastal Exploration of Washington.* Palo Alto: Pacific Books, 1959.

Yates, Steve. *Marine Wildlife of Puget Sound, the San Juans and the Strait of Georgia.* Chester, CT: The Globe Pequot Press, 1988.